ZERO LOT LINE HOUSING

by David R. Jensen/HOH Associates

the Urban Land Institute
1090 Vermont Avenue, N.W.
Washington, D.C. 20005

Recommended bibliographic listing:
David R. Jensen/HOH Associates
Zero Lot Line Housing. Washington:
Urban Land Institute, 1981.

Second Printing, 1987.

ISBN 0-87420-600-6
Library of Congress Card Catalog Number 81-40469
Printed in the United States of America

About the Author

David R. Jensen is Executive Vice President and principal in charge of planning at HOH Associates, Inc., a planning and design firm in Denver, Colorado. Since joining HOH in 1967, Jensen has had varied experience in project planning and administration for both the public and private sectors and in environmental planning.

He is a speaker at various universities and is chairman of the NAHB Committee on Land Use Policy and Design. He is a National Trustee of the American Society of Landscape Architects; a Past President of the Colorado Chapter of the ASLA; a member of the Real Estate Advisory Board, College of Business Administration at the University of Denver; and an Associate Member in the National Association of Home Builders.

Acknowledgments

At HOH, we try to perform all projects on a team basis. That has been the case with this book. The product is that of a highly skilled group with which I am fortunate to be associated. While there was some hesitancy at the outset, this team has proven its superior abilities. It would be difficult to give proper credit to all people that produced this publication. The key persons for text contributions included Brad Nelson, Duane Blossom, Mike Pharo, Gene Herbert, Tim Dreese, Steve Wilensky, Arnold Ray, and Guy Peterson. Jay Parker assisted in on-site project research; Denise Jordan in typing; Jody Newton, Joan Johnston, and Nancy Maul in graphics; and Keith McClintock and Rhoda Bliss in all aspects of research, text, proofing, and coordination. The total office could be listed.

Additionally, and extremely key to any document of this nature, the industry has been kind in providing their projects for my review. Without their time and contributions this document would be incomplete. My thanks to:

Arvida Corporation	Miami, FL
Austin Construction & Development Co.	Hilton Head, SC
Blietz Organization	Evanston, IL
Brandermill Group	Richmond, VA
Broadmoor Homes	Irvine, CA
Chism Homes	Las Vegas, NV
Conner Development Company	Bellevue, WA
Coral Ridge Properties	Coral Springs, FL
Coyle Realty	Oklahoma City, OK
Gentry Pacific, Ltd.	Honolulu, HI
Goodman, Seger, Hogan Planning Company	Virginia Beach, VA
Green Run Development Corporation	Virginia Beach, VA
Hilton Head Company	Hilton Head, SC
Hollywood, Inc.	Hollywood, FL
Howard Homes	Columbia, MD
Irvine Pacific	Newport Beach, CA
Kettler Brothers	Montgomery Village, MD
Lighthouse Realty	Hilton Head, SC
Mililani Town, Inc.	Oahu, HI
Mission Viejo Company	Mission Viejo, CA
National Building & Development Corp.	Boca Raton, FL
Nu-West Colorado, Inc.	Englewood, CO
Otto Paparazzo Management, Inc.	Farmington, CT
Peterson Associates	Virginia Beach, VA
Sandpiper Homes	Ft. Collins, CO
Showcase Development, Ltd.	Boca Raton, FL
South Coast Community Development	Dana Point, CA
Stein Brief Group	Irvine, CA
Patrick Sweet, B.E.S.; M.C.I.P.	Bramalea, Ontario, Canada
J.K. Timmons & Associates	Chesterfield County, VA
Twin Oaks Development	Hilton Head, SC

I also appreciate the assistance of Frank Spink and other ULI staff for their assistance, and a special thanks to those ULI members who reviewed the text.

About ULI-the Urban Land Institute

ULI-the Urban Land Institute is an independent, nonprofit research and educational organization incorporated in 1936 to improve the quality and standards of land use and development.

The Institute is committeed to conducting practical research in the various fields of real estate knowledge; identifying and interpreting land use trends in relation to the changing economic, social, and civic needs of the people; and disseminating pertinent information leading to the orderly and more efficient use and development of land.

ULI receives its financial support from membership dues, sale of publications, and contributions for research and panel services.

Ronald R. Rumbaugh
Executive Vice President

ULI Staff

Senior Director, Publications — Frank H. Spink, Jr.
Editor — Nadine Huff
Production Manager — Robert L. Helms
Production Assistant — Regina P. Agricola
Art Director — Carolyn de Haas

Metric Conversions

meters = feet × 0.305
kilometers = miles × 1.609
square meters = sq. ft. ×0.093
hectares = acres × 0.405
(1 hectare = 10,000 square meters)

ULI Publications Review

The strength of ULI's publications is due to the quality of authorship and the use of a review committee who is experienced with the subject, and whose review of outlines and manuscripts enhance the work of the author. The review committee for this book, drawn mostly from the Residential Council, provided guidance to the author and suggestions for clarification or expansion of coverage. Unanimity of opinion was not sought—rather a fullness of viewpoint and a reflection of views and experience from a group of knowledgeable professionals.

Contents

Foreword

In each decade since the 1940s, innovation in housing design has focused on one housing form. The decade of the '40s was the decade of shortage. Coming out of the Depression and then the Second World War, the United States was short of all housing. The suburban housing boom started in the late '40s but it was in the '50s that the mass built single-family detached house really dominated the housing scene. This housing form moved into the decade of the '60s with new concepts and innovations and refinements. The focus was on innovative land planning with open space communities, planned unit developments, and clusters being the features that set single-family housing of the '60s apart from those of the '50s. In addition, the apartment became the major focus of design innovation. The garden apartment, with its greenspace and elaborate amenities intended to attract specific markets such as the mature adult, the "swinging" single, and other submarket groups, was brought out of retirement.

The next decade saw the boom in townhouse development and design and the advent of the condominium form of ownership. The decade of the '70s also saw the beginning of trends which will affect our housing choices for the future. Land and land development costs began to rise dramatically. In the second half of the decade the seemingly unending flow of cheap energy came to a screeching halt. The rate of inflation rose dramatically, mortgage interest rates climbed, and the cost of single-family ownership began to outrun the pattern of rising incomes.

Today more and more people are being priced out of the housing market. Yet the demand for housing that will maintain the desirable characteristics of the single-family detached house remains a strong preference for a significant portion of the population. The decade of the '80s, therefore, will see a search for housing forms and designs that can accommodate new circumstances—the need to reduce per dwelling land and improvements costs, energy consumption, and maintenance demands; the necessity for households to have two incomes to support a house purchase; the need for a smaller housing unit which reflects changing demographics; and the need for housing designs suitable for infill sites where the higher densities of townhouses and apartment condominiums are inappropriate. All these needs must be balanced against a continuing desire for a house on a lot with private open space.

Measured against those criteria, zero lot line housing would seem to be a housing type that will come into its own in the '80s. ZLL is not a new idea. Like almost every contemporary housing type, it has its origins in antiquity. Isolated examples have been developed in the last 30 years throughout the United States. In 1963 ULI published *The Patio House* (Technical Bulletin 45) which suggested that the patio house or ZLL house might be an important house form within the then growing interest in planned unit development and open space community design. However, the zero lot line house did not become the dominant housing form. Instead, single-family detached housing on smaller lots was an effective response to the then modestly rising costs of housing and land development. The higher potential densities of garden apartments and townhouses came to predominate.

Why then does ZLL have such apparent merit in the 1980s? The answer would appear to lie in its response to the factors mentioned earlier while still responding to the preference for fee simple ownership of a house on a lot. That is not to say that zero lot line housing will supplant either single-family detached or townhouse condominium developments, but rather that it has become a logical alternative.

In recognition of the absence of good information on zero lot line housing and design, ULI approached David Jensen of the firm of HOH Associates to determine his interest in developing a publication on zero lot like housing. HOH was the logical firm to approach for innovation in residential land development and housing types. Twenty years ago Robert M. O'Donnell (the "O" in HOH Associates) authored ULI's *New Approaches to Residential Land Development* (Technical Bulletin 40), which was for many years the most comprehensive publication on planned unit development and innovative land planning concepts.

This book is designed to be a companion to ULI's *Planning and Design of Townhouses and Condominiums*, published in 1979. It is a collection of some of the best concepts in planning and design for zero lot line housing. It is a graphic as well as verbal book. Many of the zero lot line concepts are best described visually by sketch, photograph, or plan, and this book provides them in abundance. We believe that zero lot line housing is a housing type for the '80s and that the concepts and ideas set forth in this publication effectively applied in the field can be the basis for well-conceived and successful zero lot line development.

Frank H. Spink, Jr.
Senior Director, Publications

1 Introduction

Providing viable housing alternatives in the 1980s is going to present a whole new set of challenges. Higher densities and smaller houses will require more sensitivity to planning and design and more attention to details. The high costs of housing will make it more difficult for young couples, the retired, and the elderly to afford homes of their own. In addition, the location of housing will become more important as increased travel costs make extensive commuting less feasible.

While this book cannot provide the answers for all housing problems, it is a guide for one solution: the zero lot line (ZLL) house. ZLL is becoming a widely used form of land development in the U.S. and Canada. In California and Hawaii, it is used as a part of standard subdivision products, and in Colorado as a part of planned unit developments (PUDs). The concept has been tried in the Chicago area, and Florida projects have used ZLL as an alternative to standard products.

ZLL housing comes in a variety of formats. In its purest form and the source of the label, "zero lot line," the single-family detached dwelling unit is placed on the lot so that it sits along one or more lot lines, hence, a zero setback. Variations on this format may include the use of traditional setbacks with

1-1 Higher densities and smaller houses are going to require more sensitivity to planning and design and more attention to details. The zero lot line concept can accommodate these needs.

easements allowing the zero lot line configuration or the arrangement of minimally connected units (such as storage sheds, roof lines, or subsurface foundations but not duplexes in the pure form), with the lot line bisecting them. Local zoning requirements and market conditions may dictate which form of zero lot line development will actually be used.

The ZLL house combines features of the detached home with higher densities, thus presenting, for some markets, a more desirable product. Yet, even with higher densities, a well-designed ZLL home can provide privacy and livability equivalent to that offered in the conventional single-family home. In addition, many features of a ZLL house can conform to the needs of the future, such as conservation of energy, land, and other resources.

As the lot size is reduced, some communities may be concerned unnecessarily that lower priced may also mean lower quality products; this report will hopefully eliminate that potential misunderstanding. Regardless of price ranges, ZLL housing allows lower development costs through more efficient development and lower per-unit land costs. When more attention is given to clustering, planning and design, and customer needs, ZLL housing as a form of single-family ownership can compete easily with traditional single-family housing with respect to marketability and lifestyle.

1-2 and 1-3 Even with higher densities, a well-designed zero lot line home can provide privacy and livability equivalent to that offered in the single-family home.

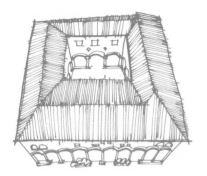

1-4 The atrium house was one of the earliest types of urban housing predominant in ancient Egypt, Greece, and Rome.

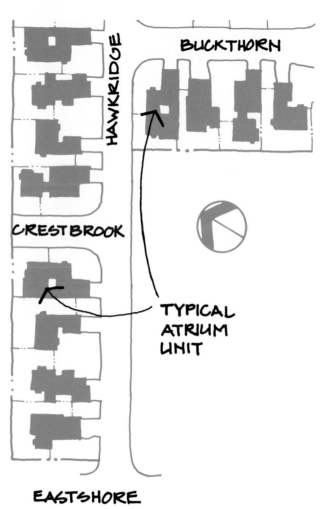

HAWKRIDGE

BUCKTHORN

CRESTBROOK

TYPICAL ATRIUM UNIT

EASTSHORE

1-5 Woodbridge Gables, Phase III, is an example of a more recent application of the atrium home in a ZLL layout.

History

The ZLL concept is not a recent innovation. Variations of it date back 4,000 years and it has been called various names, such as atrium house, patio house, or court house. The atrium house, for example, was one of the earliest types of urban housing, being predominant in ancient Egypt, Greece, and Rome. It existed as a single-family dwelling unit with one or more courts partially or completely surrounded by living areas. City sizes were restricted, and the court house provided the greatest densities at low building height.

With some regional variations, the atrium version of the ZLL house existed in Northern Africa, Mesopotamia, and the Far East. The Moorish invasion of the Iberian Penninsula may have introduced it to Spain, and Spanish colonists introduced it to Latin America, where it is a dominant dwelling type to this day.

In spite of its long history, forms of ZLL housing have not been widely accepted where they were not indigenous. Some attempts were made to introduce it to Germany and the United States after the First World War, with limited success. Modern versions were readily accepted in Tunis after the Second World War, but these housing forms had never ceased to be indigenous to that area.

Recent applications of ZLL designs have not been limited to warm climates. Since 1950, there has been successful development in northern areas, such as Denmark, Sweden, England, and Canada. Advantages that have been cited are privacy, improved residential environment, economic use of land, and adaptability to natural terrain. The ZLL concept is suitable for use in both urban or suburban environments and has proven to be an economical and logical response to high-cost infill parcels.

Trends in housing layouts leading up to the present ZLL concept probably began in the 1930s with the Radburn innovations. More direct evolution can be traced to clustering and then to the planned unit development (PUD) concept of the 1960s. At that time, grouping dwellings closer together in order to preserve open space became a much used practice. The ZLL approach came into being in order to more efficiently utilize the smaller lot resulting from the clustering.

Clustering of housing includes ZLL concepts. Custom ZLL homes are being built in diverse locations and for diverse markets—as second homes in Hilton Head Island, South Carolina; as clusters in Florida; or as standard lot subdivisions in California. ZLL is an opportunity to create a better residential environment than in past practices. The key is attention to overall planning, design, and consumer needs on all price levels.

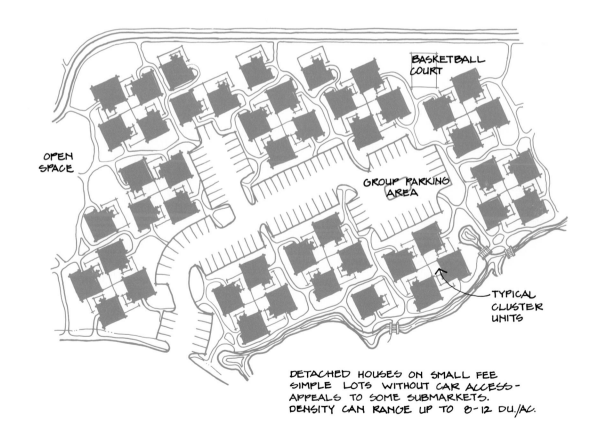

BASKETBALL COURT

OPEN SPACE

GROUP PARKING AREA

TYPICAL CLUSTER UNITS

DETACHED HOUSES ON SMALL FEE SIMPLE LOTS WITHOUT CAR ACCESS - APPEALS TO SOME SUBMARKETS. DENSITY CAN RANGE UP TO 8-12 DU./AC.

1-6   ZLL was established to use more efficiently the smaller lot resulting from clustering.

5

ZLL Housing in the Future

Several current trends are likely to contribute to the popularity and the acceptability of ZLL housing in the future. Increasing housing costs and the unavailability of moderately priced housing is causing social and ethnic isolation. This trend is likely to continue as long as housing cost increases exceed income increases. ZLL housing can improve the stability and quality of neighborhoods by providing more affordable housing for a wider range of incomes.

The trend toward smaller family sizes, with couples having only one child or even no children, decreases the need for every home to have a large yard. With more women pursuing professional goals, this trend will continue. ZLL, combined with clustering, allows excess yards to be combined into usable open space. Also, the addition of more lots allows lower per-unit costs. Overall, the U.S. population is maturing and the predominately single-level design of ZLL will be attrac-

1-7 Direct evolution can be traced to clustering and then to the planned unit development concept of the 1960s.

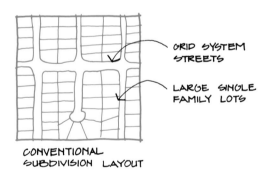

GRID SYSTEM STREETS

LARGE SINGLE FAMILY LOTS

CONVENTIONAL SUBDIVISION LAYOUT

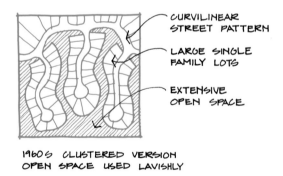

CURVILINEAR STREET PATTERN

LARGE SINGLE FAMILY LOTS

EXTENSIVE OPEN SPACE

1960S CLUSTERED VERSION OPEN SPACE USED LAVISHLY

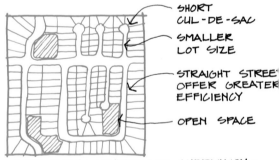

SHORT CUL-DE-SAC

SMALLER LOT SIZE

STRAIGHT STREET OFFER GREATER EFFICIENCY

OPEN SPACE

LATE 1970S; MINIMAL LOT SUBDIVISION — MORE RESTRAINED USE OF COMMON OPEN AREAS — MORE EMPHASIS ON LIVABILITY OF SMALLER LOTS.
(QUALITY OF INWARD SPACE)

tive to mature markets. Money saved in land and development costs can be used to reduce the sales price of the house or to include extra features within the house or overall development.

Energy conservation, an important issue in our society, can be achieved in a variety of ways with ZLL development. Shorter, and possibly narrower, streets require less petroleum-based raw material; in addition, less

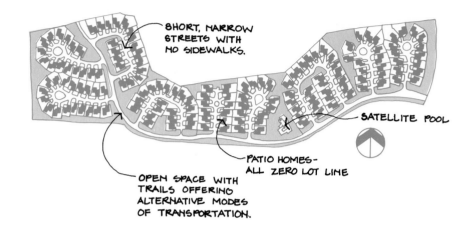

SHORT, NARROW STREETS WITH NO SIDEWALKS.

SATELLITE POOL

PATIO HOMES - ALL ZERO LOT LINE

OPEN SPACE WITH TRAILS OFFERING ALTERNATIVE MODES OF TRANSPORTATION.

1-8 Shorter and narrower streets without sidewalks require less raw materials and reduced energy in the construction process.
1-9 Also, well-planned open space with trails linking units to amenities offers alternative modes of transportation. These concepts are demonstrated in The Crossings development in Dade County, Florida.

1-10 Glass areas opening onto private side yards and courts can visually expand the living areas of ZLL homes. 1-11 and 1-12 The expanded living areas can be used for dining or relaxing.

energy is used in the construction process. Automobile travel distances are reduced, thus saving considerable fuel over the long term. Well-planned developments encourage alternative transportation modes, such as walking or biking to schools, recreation, and shopping, which saves even more fuel.

The homes themselves are considerably more energy efficient. With at least one blank wall (no windows or openings), loss of heat is reduced. Most of the windows face onto the enclosed spaces, where they are protected from harsh winter winds and from brilliant summer sun by overhangs. Since windows tend to open onto the enclosed spaces, which are both private and secure, glass doors and windows can be left open to capture summer breezes. Problems with dust are lessened because of the protection

of the walls. Enclosed spaces provide a protected micro-climate where the extremes of
climate are lessened and this, in turn, influences the climate within the house.

Homes are visually extended into the courtyard, and courtyards into the houses, so
even relatively modest homes need not
appear small. The courtyard itself provides
additional living space, allowing for dining,
sunbathing, or relaxing in complete privacy.

ZLL is applicable to any size lot where efficiency is derived within the lot; 50- and 55-
foot-wide lots with unit sizes varying from 35
feet to 20 feet are prevalent. The average
width is likely to be reduced with consumer
acceptance and improved design and use.
While the ZLL concept is mostly used on
smaller lots, it can be used for all lot sizes.

2 Zero Lot Line Housing

ZLL housing is simply moving the house onto the adjacent property line as shown in Figure 2-2. It has basic derivations, though. The most common is the placement of the home three to five feet from the adjacent property line. The intention is two-fold: the first is to avoid having to provide access easements across the adjacent lot (this is not a problem and is easily provided for; see Appendix A); the second, and by far the most important, is to avoid added costs for fire protection caused by placing the wall directly on the property line. Building codes usually require increases to one- or two-hour fire ratings even though the minimum required building separation occurs. Attempts are being made to eliminate this increase in cost just because the wall is placed on the lot line.

2-1   ZLL housing does not need to appear significantly different than conventional single-family housing. It can appeal to all market ranges and lifestyles.

Another derivation of the ZLL concept is a departure from the standard single-family layout. This would resemble most closely a condominium type ownership where lot is limited to the land directly below the building and patio and may not front on a street. Access may be from a common parking or garage area.

Some forms of ZLL result from circumvention of local standards and codes. Where setbacks in single-family areas are too large and inflexible, ZLL concepts have been achieved through duplex or multifamily zoning while retaining the single-family image. Connections between structures are disguised and made through storage sheds, below-grade foundations, shade structures, or similar gimmicks to avoid inflexible regulations.

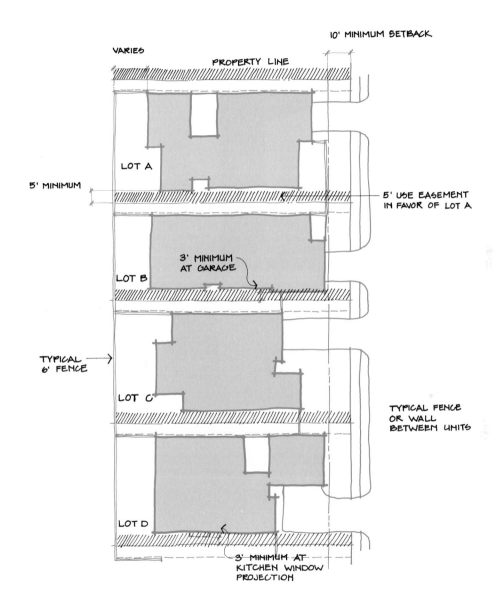

2-2   ZLL is simply moving the house onto the adjacent property line. The most common variation is the placement of the house three to five feet from the adjacent property line and the provision of a use easement along that side of the unit.

2-3   Building codes often require that no openings occur on the "on-the-line" wall. 2-4   This provides privacy and the opportunity to utilize that wall as a backdrop for landscaping.   2-5   However, with careful design, some openings could be permitted for light or ventilation without jeopardizing privacy.

For privacy, the "on-the-line" wall normally is planned without any openings. Often, local building codes will preclude such openings. However, in some jurisdictions high first- and second-story windows may be used, which permit light and air circulation but maintain privacy and reduce noise. This solid wall provides privacy by allowing the adjacent house to be opened up through use of glass doors and windows, providing visual expansion and natural lighting of the interior. Outside yards also gain in privacy, by being separated in most instances by walls or fencing.

Glass areas for light and passive solar collection can be more functional for the dwelling interior through attention to street and unit siting concepts. The ZLL dwelling usually implies a directional window orientation. Assuming the typical ZLL dwelling consolidates the glass on one side of the house, this can be ideal for passive solar gain.

Price-value influences determine the use of the side yard. For instance, ZLL housing is most commonly suited for "lifestyle" markets as well as shelter markets. In most instances, the shelter market, where high-quality open space development is not economically feasible, will benefit from the ZLL concept.

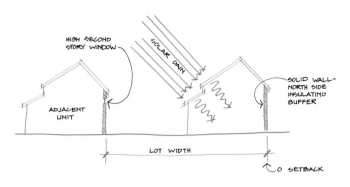

2-6   The ZLL dwelling usually implies a directional window orientation. In colder climates, windows are generally oriented to the south, allowing the sun to penetrate into the unit. In hot desert climates, the windows may be oriented to the north, away from the sun.

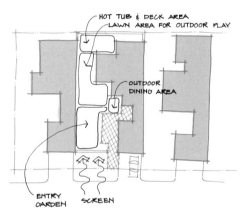

2-8   Price-value influences determine the use of the side yard. In some markets, the homeowner is looking for outdoor entertainment areas and perhaps a pool. 2-9   In other markets, the homeowner seeks storage space and work areas.

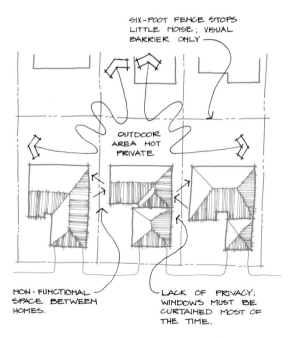

2-7   As economic pressures force narrower and narrower lots, use of side yards becomes limited. Windows located close to the windows of adjacent houses reduce privacy between units.

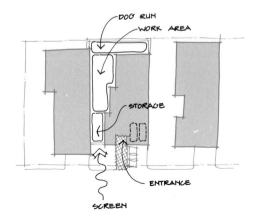

13

Site Influences

One of the premises of the cluster principle is to cluster units in areas of the site with the most developable slopes in order to have less topographic impact. Land use areas for smaller lot developments should be located on the flattest land possible. A common fallacy is that the site containing rough terrain can be developed with less cost for grading if the units are clustered. This can be true if rough terrain is avoided and more "buildable" parts of the site are not designed high in density. Often rough terrain sites contain ridge tops and hillsides which are "buildable" only by comparison. As much as a four to five percent cross slope can significantly impact the cost of con-

structing ZLL dwellings on small lots because retaining walls between lots or extra tall foundation walls on units will be required. Generally, sites with over three percent cross slopes will necessitate some adaptive design for lot grading.

Particular care should be taken in selecting sites for use of ZLL on small lots. Instead of forcing a concept onto a site, another site that is more suitable should be selected. Where ZLL on small lots appears unsuited due to cost or terrain, alternative development on larger lots or on lots designed for tightly clustered multifamily housing should be considered.

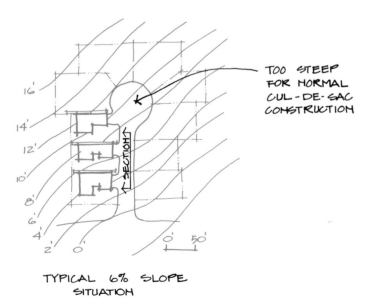

TOO STEEP FOR NORMAL CUL-DE-SAC CONSTRUCTION

TYPICAL 6% SLOPE SITUATION

2-10 and 2-11 Often rough terrain sites contain ridge tops and hillsides which are "buildable" by comparison. Even the slightest of slopes can result in higher building costs per unit. Steeper slopes become unbuildable only from a cost standpoint.

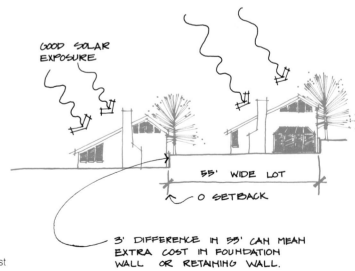

GOOD SOLAR EXPOSURE

55' WIDE LOT

O SETBACK

3' DIFFERENCE IN 55' CAN MEAN EXTRA COST IN FOUNDATION WALL OR RETAINING WALL.

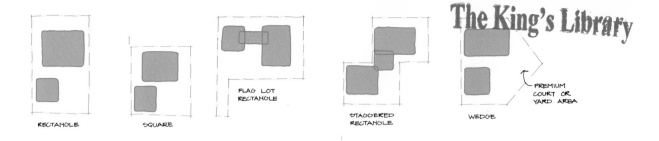

RECTANGLE   SQUARE   FLAG LOT RECTANGLE   STAGGERED RECTANGLE   WEDGE   PREMIUM COURT OR YARD AREA

Lot Configurations

As is the case with conventional lots, the rectangular form is the most used shape for ZLL homes. Various sized rectangles can be grouped in a very efficient manner to maximize usage of the land. Alternative forms may include a square, which basically functions on the same principle as a rectangle but, for architectural reasons, requires dimensional changes. Wedges, or five-sided pie-shaped lots, are usually kept to a minimum due to site utilization considerations. These lots are usually located at the bend in a road or cul-de-sac ends and should be considered premium lots due to the increase in size. Occasionally, and more prevalent in small lots, there is reason to provide for a staggered rectangle in order to accommodate an architectural concept. These lots are then fit together to form a harmonious architectural cluster. All of the shapes may be modified slightly on one or more edges by curved right-of-way line influences or by parcel lines which do not run parallel or perpendicular to streets.

It is undesirable to plat lots in ZLL programs before or apart from the architectural design of the individual dwellings, particularly for small lot projects. It limits design in some cases or causes repetition in others. An alternative is to design and site the architectural product and then draw the lot lines. The developer should plat only the number he is confident of building before the market changes, though local conditions or processing may warrant other actions. Ideally, no more should be platted than can be absorbed in two years.

2-12 The rectangular form is the most common lot shape for ZLL homes, however, various rectangular modifications may be used.
2-13 At Broadmoor Woodbridge Cottages, Irvine, California, the rectangular lot configuration was used, yielding a very high density.

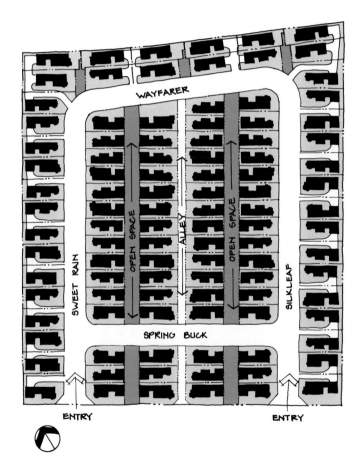

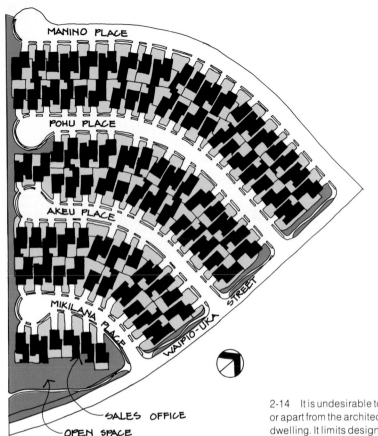

MANINO PLACE
POHU PLACE
AKEU PLACE
MIKILANA PLACE
WAIPIO-UKA STREET

— SALES OFFICE
— OPEN SPACE

Flexibility in lot lines is important. Lot lines do not need to be perpendicular to the street or, in some cases, be attached to streets. Nor do they need to be the same width, size, or shape. For example, zig-zag, staggered, or variable lot lines may offer the most functional shape for some extremely small lot programs for the house and yard functions, but should be carefully considered before recording. When platting lots, allowances for future additions by the homeowner will appeal to some markets and provide expansion potential to the homebuyer. The rear end of the lot frequently can be designed for this. Extra lot depth can sometimes be designed without the large reduction in density that extra widths would cause.

2-14 It is undesirable to plat lots in ZLL programs before or apart from the architectural design of the individual dwelling. It limits design in some cases or causes repetition in others. At Waipio by Gentry (in Oahu, Hawaii), the unit shapes create the outdoor spaces rather than lot lines. In this development the lot lines play a very minor role compared to the design of the unit.

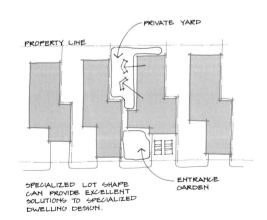

PRIVATE YARD
PROPERTY LINE
SPECIALIZED LOT SHAPE CAN PROVIDE EXCELLENT SOLUTIONS TO SPECIALIZED DWELLING DESIGN.
ENTRANCE GARDEN

2-15 Zig-zag, staggered, or variable lot lines may offer the most functional shape for some extremely small lot programs. Notice that the units are not all exactly alike even though they all fit the same zig-zag lot line. This alternative also yields some of the best areas for outdoor use since the spaces are broken up and not all in one area.

Easements

Easements in ZLL may be classified as follows:

- drainage
- maintenance/access/use
- utility
- landscaping
- building setback
- solar
- view preservation

As in conventional development, not all of these easements are required in every instance. Also, one or more of these easements may occur in the same area, but probably for different reasons. In contrast to conventional development, some of these easements may occur in the common areas, rather than on individual lots, due to the size of the lots.

- **Drainage easements** may occur in two locations: 1) between lots for the purpose of allowing runoff from the street to exit a cluster, or 2) on each lot to allow runoff from adjacent roofs and private yards to exit the yard. When the building wall is set off the property line, the easement is normally centered on the property line as in conventional projects. Drainage easements between lots can be five to 15 feet wide and may occupy the same area as a pedestrian walkway. Easements on lots are normally smaller, often two to 10 feet in width.

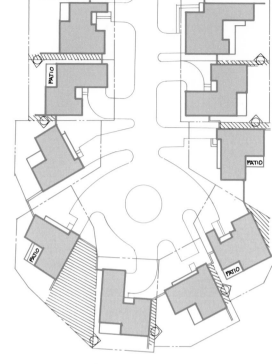

2-16 Use easements are often utilized in zero lot line developments as shown here at Country Walk Patio Homes in Dade County, Florida. Notice that not all lots have a use easement.

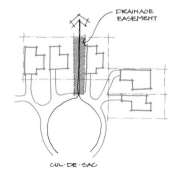

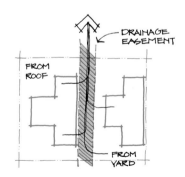

2-17 Drainage easements may occur in two locations: between lots for the purpose of allowing runoff from the street to exit cluster or 2-18 on each lot to allow runoff from adjacent roofs and private yards to exit the yards.

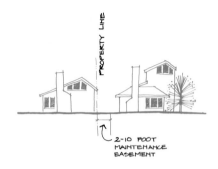

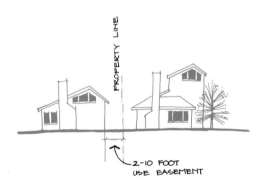

2-19 Maintenance easements may be required to provide the homeowner the right to enter adjacent property in order to service the side of his home that is located on the lot line.

2-20 In some instances, the home is set back two to 10 feet from the lot line so access can occur on each lot. This area is then utilized as a use easement.

- **Maintenance/access/use easements** may be required to provide a homeowner the right to enter adjacent property to service the side of his home located on the lot line or to have access for use (see Appendix A). Widths of these easements can be two to 10 feet, depending on codes or project requirements. These easements are often combined with covenants limiting any use which could physically preclude access to areas along the ZLL wall. Provision for maintenance or access is handled in deed restrictions (see Appendix A). An alternative to having an easement on the adjacent lot is to set back the dwelling unit two to five feet from the lot line so access can occur on each lot, and then give the adjacent lot use of this area through an easement on the setback area.

- **Utility easements** occur in the same manner as in conventional development, although emphasis is placed on three options: (1) to locate all utilities in the front, (2) to locate all utilities in the rear, or (3) to locate them in side yards. When a project has a common area at the rear of lots, a more conventional approach is possible because room is provided in which to locate the utilities. Conventional rear easements are five to 10 feet. When no common area touches each lot, the first option becomes very important. Again, the small size of the lots tends to force major easements to occur either in public or common areas. An easement may be used for common service lines to more than one lot and occur in and with other easements.

2-21 An easement may be used for common service lines for more than one lot and occur in and with other easements. Utility easements for power and phone generally occur in the rear of the lot while service easements for water and sewer lines usually occur in the front of the units.

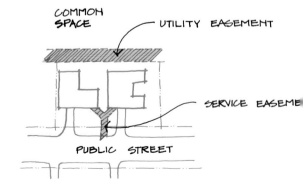

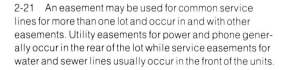

- **Landscaping easements** are not commonly used in standard subdivisions, but can be very useful in higher density projects such as ZLL in providing much needed continuity and project identity. Landscape easements provide that certain areas, such as building setbacks or right-of-ways, will be set aside and maintained in landscaping. Fences must be set back of the easement and even number and type of plants may be specified. Sometimes these areas may be landscaped by the developer, which can be especially useful as a marketing tool in higher density projects. In other cases, the covenants may specify time limits within which the resident must install the landscaping.

- **Building setback easements** can apply to each lot in a manner unique to each project. Allowable setbacks are usually determined at the time of plan approval and are variable. Of primary importance are the setbacks from streets, both from the standpoint of safety and aesthetics. Setbacks vary considerably depending upon the planning and architectural program, but in general the garage door should be kept to less than five feet or more than 18 feet from the back of the front sidewalk. Distances between five to 18 feet can block the sidewalk if the driveway is used for parking. Aesthetics may make desirable setbacks less than 18 feet.

Rear setbacks should be as needed depending on location of additional structures. Some ZLL projects have walls on both the side and rear lot lines. The structure may touch the rear line if next to a common area or if placement of adjacent structures will allow. Side yards require consideration of the adjacent building locations. The Uniform Building Code presently requires a minimum of three feet between building and lot line using residential frame construction. Building on the line usually requires additional fire proofing.

2-22 Landscape easements provide that certain areas such as building setbacks or rights-of-way will be set aside and maintained in landscaping. Sometimes the setback requirements imposed upon a parcel will not allow for zero lot line homes unless special measures are taken.

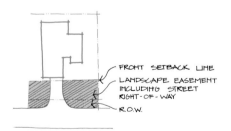

FRONT SETBACK LINE
LANDSCAPE EASEMENT INCLUDING STREET RIGHT-OF-WAY
R.O.W.

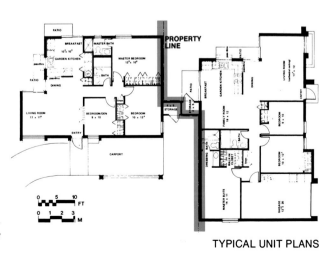

PROPERTY LINE

TYPICAL UNIT PLANS

2-23 At Shadow Wood, Coral Springs, Florida, the setback restrictions were avoided by attaching units with storage sheds.

REAR SETBACK POTENTIAL DEPENDING UPON NEARNESS OF ADJACENT BUILDINGS (O FEET REQUIRED IF ON COMMONS; 3-5 FEET REQUIRED OTHERWISE).

SIDE YARD SETBACK - O FEET ON ONE SIDE

SIDE YARD POTENTIAL DEPENDING UPON ARCHITECTURAL/YARD REQUIREMENTS (3-5 FEET NORMALLY).

FRONT SETBACK POTENTIAL DEPENDING UPON PARKING PROVISIONS & STREETSCAPE (10-18 FEET NORMALLY).

2-24 Setbacks vary considerably depending upon the planning and architectural program.

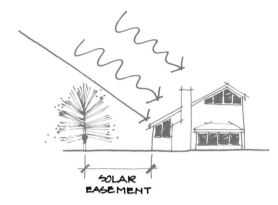

2-25 Building orientation and heights, roof planes, and location of vegetation must be considered to ensure maximum solar access for units.

● **Solar easements** are extremely specialized. Obviously, consideration of such easements is related to those structures which are supplied in part or whole by a solar heating system. Basically, limitations on building orientation, building heights, roof planes, and plant material sizing and locations are involved in relationship to heights and seasonal sun angles. However, sufficient variables exist in terms of regional location and systems, making any blanket suggestions very difficult. It is suggested that any project whose program requires solar considerations be reviewed by a solar systems specialist.

● **View preservation easements** can be implemented on a project-wide basis, on a phase basis, or a selective lot basis. These easements can occur in horizontal planes (relating to structure placement), or in the vertical planes (relating to structure or landscaping height). Attempts should be made to design the lotting configuration to allow view corridors between buildings. Controls on architectural height and plant material placement and height must also be implemented to insure success. A very strong and thorough design review process is encouraged to manage such a program.

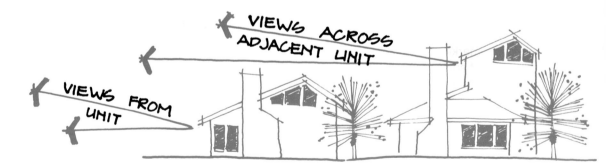

2-26 Controls on architectural height and plant material placement and height must be implemented to insure success of view preservation easements.

Common Areas

Common area refers to the land held in common ownership by the residents of the project. Common area can also be termed open space, greenspace, or private park, and may include planted islands, park strips, and similar areas. The extent of common area in a ZLL project depends upon the amount of property which must be preserved due to physiographic constraints, the desired extent of linkages, the extent of physical recreation or visual amenities, the cost, and consumer needs. Care should be taken to analyze the common area program in terms of balance between the number of lots and amount of common area, the requirements of future residents plus the community to develop the common area, and the requirements and cost to continually maintain the common area. Certain programs may require absolutely no common area; others may have extensive common area. The extent of common area should be a function of the development economics, market demand, or user preference, and not solely of how many units there are to support the maintenance fees.

Common areas, if planned, may be used to locate major recreation facilities such as a clubhouse, pool, or court games, which cannot be located on individual lots. They may be in the form of linkages which connect various elements of a project together via pedestrian and bike trails. Severe topography, dense vegetation, drainage courses, or other significant natural features may be the basis for a preservation or conservation common area. Increasingly, there is a trend to avoid a common area which is composed only of "leftover" space. Leftover refers not to preservation or conservation areas, but rather to odd-shaped areas which cannot be efficiently lotted. This type of area serves no real purpose as open space since it is often isolated or difficult to physically or visually use and is often a maintenance burden due to awkward slopes and nonefficient irrigation requirements. Most programs benefit by providing landscaped space where a visual amenity is required; isolated or awkward parcels are prorated into adjacent lots and thus become an asset (increased lot size) to the residents.

2-27, 2-28, and 2-29 Common areas can be in the form of open space, greenspace, or private parks, and may include planted islands, park strips, or recreation facilities.

A recent trend is to shift from "backyard" open space with its long inefficient linkages to parks and larger open space areas, centrally located for easy front door access and viewing. It should be noted that going to small lots is not an automatic indication that open space is required (although many zoning ordinances require a percentage of open common area). Instead, open space and recreation facilities should be provided, but balanced with the project costs, needs of residents, concept of the project, and availability of facilities in the project vicinity. Project planning should be for and responsive to future resident needs, not standard regulations.

Private Spaces

Private spaces are the "yard" areas of each lot. The yards are formed by the walls of the structures (two on-site and usually at least one off-site) and by the fences or walls which connect with the structures. Depending upon lot size and layout of structures, the lots do not have to be completely enclosed. Partial and minimum fencing can provide the required privacy and, in addition, a sense of openness and lower cost.

Ideally, these yard areas are considered extensions of the interior living spaces. When connected by doorways, the yards become patios or courtyards, often with a special character and purpose such as an entry court or sitting area. Larger ZLL lots will be more conducive to conventional grassed yards. In ZLL the norm is more often a design of paving and plant materials which provide low maintenance use areas.

2-30, 2-31, and 2-32 Common areas, if planned properly, may be used to locate major recreational facilities such as a clubhouse, pool, or court games, and may be in the form of linkages such as pedestrian and bike trails.

2-33 and 2-34 Ideally, courtyards are considered extensions of the interior living space and should be developed to provide privacy and pleasant surroundings. Attention must be paid to details such as use of materials, ground cover, and solar orientation.

Private/Common Area Relationship

Ideally, private yard areas and common areas should relate in such a manner as to be indistinguishable if they are adjacent or have some commonality, from a visual standpoint. To accomplish this, landscape development (i.e. fencing or plant materials) and intensity should be uniform between the two areas. Too often, fencing is incorporated for security reasons, which isolates or segregates the common area from the private yard and in doing so creates an unharmonious visual barrier and limits access and use. Only if the intensity of the landscape is equalized on both sides of the fence will the project flow visually and present a sense of continuity.

Care needs to be taken in the placement of open space to avoid security problems through creating too many "public" edges to the lots. The backyard open space linkage is an example of increasing potential security edges and adding significant project costs for fencing, lighting, landscaping, paths, and long-term maintenance.

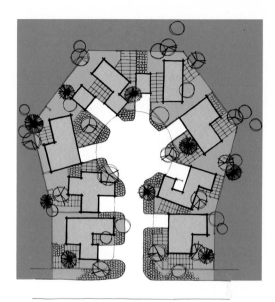

2-35 Ideally, private yard areas and common areas should relate in such a manner as to be indistinguishable if they are adjacent. To accomplish this, the landscape development and intensity should be uniform between the two areas. Notice that the open space seems to flow into the yards of these cluster homes at Lansbrook, Oklahoma City, Oklahoma.

3 Site Selection Considerations

There are obvious aspects which affect the sales price and cost of housing, such as cost of materials and services. These cost elements are automatically taken into consideration during the planning stages of any project. Not so obvious are the aspects of site planning discussed here. Site planning considerations for a ZLL project are much the same as for the standard subdivision, although, generally, higher density use causes site considerations to take on even more importance. Besides the natural aspects, there are also man-made considerations, such as access, utility availability and capacity, proximity of parks and schools, processing time and requirements, and surrounding land usage. Prior to site acquisition, adequate studies should be conducted to determine physical development suitability, political feasibility, and economic opportunities.

3-1 ZLL houses can be developed in a variety of styles, depending on regional differences, climates, and site conditions.

Natural/Man-Made Influences

One aspect of choosing the proper site for ZLL development involves the careful evaluation of the area's natural and man-made influences.

As with most housing types, the proposed ZLL site should be as flat as possible with slopes under five percent to minimize grading, use of retaining walls, and other high-cost construction. Steeper or more rolling terrain should be reserved for another land use, for common open space areas, for buffer zones to separate different uses, or for adding visual interest to the area. Although some architectural solutions and innovative construction techniques might overcome steeper slope constraints, the higher costs might not meet the anticipated market objectives of the ZLL concept. Some ideas on economical architectural alternatives might be helpful and these are covered in the Building Design section (p.72). In higher price ranges, interest can be created by using the slopes through stepping the buildings, improving views, and creating more diversity.

South-facing slopes should be considered for passive and active solar use, with patios, courtyards, and living areas oriented to maximize southern exposures. While not as efficient, north-facing slopes can be designed to maximize solar gain. A site not offering generally flat terrain with potential for southern exposure to at least some part of each lot demands a more innovative approach to satisfying solar use requirements. All slope aspects require attention to street, building, and roof orientation considerations. It has been well documented that projects on north-facing slopes use more energy for heating than identical ones on south-facing slopes.

3-2 Steeper or more rolling terrain should be reserved for other land uses, common open space areas, buffer zones to separate different uses, or visual interest. As shown in this plan of Regatta Pointe, Chesterfield County, Virginia, the open space provided not only takes up areas of steep slopes and floodplains along the Swift Creek Reservoir, but also provides buffer zones, linkages, islands, and entry plantings.

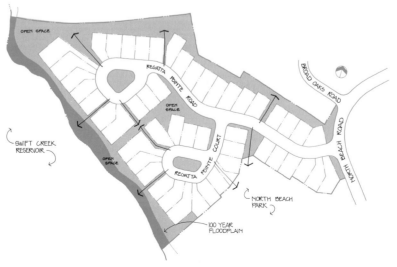

25

Soils/Geology/Groundwater

As with any residential development program, sites within floodplain designations, natural hazard areas such as earthquake zones, or other soils/geologic related limitations should be carefully scrutinized. Although development could proceed in most cases, depending upon regulations, extremely high construction costs to mitigate geologic constraints might prohibit ZLL consideration. Net usable, versus gross, site acreage is most important when looking at site suitability.

Research on previous uses of the site should be done to ascertain if past use makes the site nonviable for the proposed housing. Situations such as landfill areas or underground mining that have been abandoned can both cause problems of gas releases and land collapse. Soil borings and historical research could prove invaluable in avoiding some problems.

The soils analysis is an important design factor. Borings should be taken following general geologic studies in typical key locations to avoid possible future surprises in development costs. These could be utility installation in bedrock areas, shrink-swell potential, bad soils, or basement excavation in high watertable areas. (The Soil Conservation Service has general information on most areas.) Underground water aquifers of impermeable shale could be a hindrance in basement design. Landslide or slippage can be noted by soils analysis and borings when a detailed site development plan is generated and building sites are determined.

Prior to final site selection, a detailed analysis of site slope and drainage features should be completed. Very often slope and drainage information are analyzed simultaneously, since the problems and solutions for both are usually interrelated. Slope analysis should include ridge lines, high and low points, and slope breakdown, such as 0-3 percent, 3-5 percent, 5-8 percent, 8-15 percent, and greater than 15 percent, depending upon local standards for construction. Also, a designation of north- and south-facing slopes is important to site design considerations, and a solar index diagram is usually very helpful. Site water movement information that should be considered includes drainage channels, streams, aquifer outlets, potential ponding areas, and historic waterways. Low areas that are characteristically wet should be noted and explored as to their extent, potential for control, and site feature possibilities. Ponding areas can be used for water control and for a site feature. All relative watertables should be designated and elevations noted for their restrictions on basement floor elevations. Soil analysis reports should have inventoried these factors. Analysis of drainage patterns

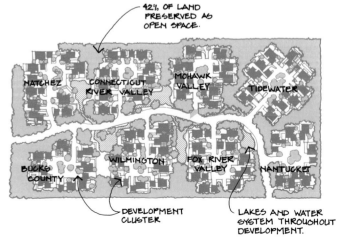

3-3 Ponding areas can be used for water control and for a site feature. This plan of Wood Creek Courts, Lincolnshire, Illinois, is an example of a well-integrated water feature. Notice the staggered rear lot lines to avoid a feeling of "alley" between clusters.

will help decide the need for detention/retention ponds. Recreation potential is high on a pond that can be recharged to retain a usable water level, but watch out for those ponds that can be a liability to future homeowners and subject to litigation.

Off-site water use and disposal has a direct effect on any site design. The overall drainage basin in which the site is included should be mapped and any future development upstream observed for impact on the site. Major changes in runoff quantities could cause problems on downstream development by increasing the amount of runoff travelling across the site and having to be retained or exited from the site. The need for on-site ponding could be determined by the quantities of impervious surface created by development. Also, the potential impact from the water exiting the site on downstream sites needs to be considered.

Disposal by evaporation, storm sewer, stream, lake, or pond should be explored, and one or all could be the solution. Lakes or visual features can be used for the benefit of site identity if a pond, stream, or other water feature is used for on-site exit/disposal. Information on 50- to 100-year floodplains should be obtained from local authorities or independent site studies. These flood zones should be noted on an analysis map and relative uses indicated for these zones. Generally, local ordinances will determine uses

within these areas, but common sense can denote open space, utility easements, or recreation oriented uses within the flood zones. When disposal of runoff water is determined, the quantity of water should also be calculated. This will help determine the type of drainage and its size. In all cases, the drainage structure should have the capacity to handle the expected water levels and include an alternative water route, should capacity exceed the expected potential. Drainage structures do not necessarily have to resemble storm sewer inlets. Potential exists, and should be explored, to utilize other forms of water runoff in order to enhance or accent the overall aesthetic appeal of the development.

With respect to downstream development, the potential for on-site erosion increases or decreases with the density. Soil analysis will reveal the composition of on-site soils. The potential of soil erosion is related to the existing vegetation and the potential for reestablishment after construction. Waterways can be utilized when major drainage conditions on and off site warrant control of drainage waters. These waterways can be used as a site amenity as well as a utilitarian feature. Areas of major erosion potential should be noted on an analysis map and means for erosion deterrents explored. The cost to reestablish growth on steep slopes or poor soils can be significant.

3-4 Low or naturally wet areas within a development can be utilized as site features. This lake in a greenbelt area provides a pleasant amenity while retaining runoff.

Unique Features

The existence of unique features should be evaluated by the potential land buyer as they relate to an overall master plan concept and governmental processing requirements. If adequate space is available for development on other portions of the site, unique features can become the basis for open space and/or amenity programs. In some cases, as with a pond or lake, residential unit clusters can be oriented to the unique feature, capitalizing on its aesthetic qualities without decreasing the land area physically suitable for development. If the site's uniqueness has been recognized by the local government, chances for successful processing and development approval might seriously be decreased.

Cultural Features

The proposed development should be compatible with adjacent land uses. Decisions need to be made as to whether surrounding land should be screened or used to the advantage of the project. Open space provided by an adjacent park or golf course could provide a more spacious feeling for the higher density ZLL projects. Ways should be investigated to link desirable features with the development. Adjacent uses such as parks, tennis courts, or lakes should not be duplicated within the project. The surrounding facilities should be utilized to save valuable developable land or to provide additional amenities. Residents or the developer of cluster or smaller lot ZLL projects should not be required to put in or maintain more facilities than comparable lower density projects on a per-unit basis.

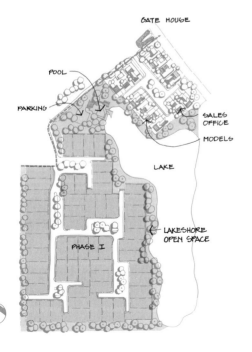

3-5 If adequate space is available for development on other portions of the site, unique features can become the basis for open space and/or amenity programs. In Pradera in Boca Raton, Florida, the lakeshore area is utilized as open space with the major recreation center also on the lake.

Regional and local access is an important consideration in site selection. The entry to the project must provide an identity matched to the project and consumer profile. For ZLL projects, local and regional bike routes and hiking trails can provide linkages to streams, aquaducts, and pedestrian areas as well as schools, shopping, and cultural features.

If old settlements of historic prominence occurred on the property, any remaining artifacts should be evaluated for preservation or restoration as they may have historic value and richness which will appeal to many buyers. Research into historic records at the county or state historic museum or society could uncover an interesting bit of past history. Logos, advertisements, and sales accents could be developed from the research. Archaeologic research early in the planning of the project will eliminate delays once construction has begun and clues to history will not be lost. Some important public relations may occur for the project.

3-7 The Upland Green development utilizes a community natural area and links this feature to the dwelling units with a series of trails.

3-8 and 3-9 The project entry must provide an identity matched to the project and consumer profile. These examples from Boca West in Palm Beach County and Country Walk in Dade County show interesting uses of materials and natural features in the project entry.

3-6 Open space provided by an adjacent park or golf course can provide a more spacious feeling for higher density ZLL projects. The surrounding facilities should be utilized to save valuable developable land or to provide additional amenities. As shown here at Cottonwood Creek, the major open space in the center of the development links up with a city park.

Visual Quality

Aesthetics should play a major role in the master site planning and marketing efforts for the ZLL developments. An initial evaluation of the site's visual quality and the impact of surrounding uses on that quality are major considerations for site analysis and selection. Although architectural innovations can add to existing visual quality aspects, these natural elements will create a pleasing and more marketable product without added cost.

Some elements of visual quality to be considered during the site selection process include variety of vegetation, steepness of slope, unique features, variety in the land form, water, and views. The more diverse these elements, generally the higher the visual quality and saleability. Although these elements are important on-site considerations, adjacent land uses also influence the visual quality of a property. Any negative elements, such as low quality housing, unsightly junk yards, or other incompatible land uses should also be considered. Major access routes should be analyzed for negative or positive impacts.

Vegetation/Wildlife

A general investigation of existing vegetation and wildlife habitats will aid the developer in determining visual appeal to potential buyers, opportunities for open space and other amenities, and potential impact from development. A site offering a variety of mature trees, shrubs, meadows, riparian areas, or unique plant types provides the developer with a "built-in" environment. Without these natural features, major landscape programs might be required to overcome deficiencies in, or improve upon, existing conditions. Although some vegetation will be eliminated for building sites and roadways, careful site planning can provide for entrance features, buffers and screening, open space, backdrops, courtyards, streetscapes, and other natural amenities, all of which utilize existing vegetation.

Overall development suitability of a potential site should consider vegetation and wildlife characteristics. The significance and location of these features will affect the number and location of dwellings, road layouts, and other land uses. In addition, processing agencies might base their approval decisions on the environmental impact of the proposed development. This aspect becomes very important during the processing stages and might, depending on the uniqueness of vegetation and/or wildlife and the policies of the processing agency, delay or decrease chances for development approval. Clustered ZLL units may allow sensitive wildlife or vegetation areas to be protected and thus avoid delays in project approval.

An inventory of existing plant material also gives a good indication of what will grow on the site, and a soils analysis will help in identifying growth potential. An inventory of types and sizes of trees generally should be made for future reference. When the detailed site design has begun, more exact locations of sizes and types can be made to determine the savable trees. Each large tree is worth thousands of dollars to a project to replace. During the development process, tree masses should be preserved intact as much as possible, as they add to the site's aesthetic quality in post development stages. Vegetation moderates the extremes of weather conditions; it is well documented that trees will reduce the amount of energy used both in summer and winter. Vegetation that is retained gives the project early visual maturity while serving as a wind screen.

Land Titles, Surveys

A comprehensive inventory of land titles and a detailed site survey will help determine the buildable land area or any disputed boundaries and easements. These points will need to be solved prior to any detailed site design. A clear deed of any claims to the property by others should be obtained to avoid long court battles. A boundary survey prior to planning is important to avoid later design changes. This is equally important for small as well as large sites. On a small site, differences in parcel shape may have a major impact on the design layout of ZLL.

Utilities

Existing storm, sanitary sewers, water, gas, and electrical services should be located and evaluated as to size, capacity, expansion potential, location, easement width, manholes, and elevation. Also, the capacity of treatment facilities is important. Utility access is important to detached homes, and provisions need to be made in the design for utility locations down a common easement/ open space or under streets. Research should determine if more innovative and cost effective solutions can be made. The processing stage is normally too late for new ideas. If adequate service facilities are not available from existing systems, or if future potential is limited, the site should not be considered further.

3-10 and 3-11 ZLL can be developed retaining much of the existing vegetation. This was especially important on Hilton Head Island, where a lifestyle market was being attracted. Existing trees were preserved within a few feet of the dwellings, providing additional privacy.

Community Services

If the ZLL concept is being utilized to obtain high densities, such as in infill situations or for low-cost housing, the availability of adjacent community services can be a very important aspect. Since the higher densities may preclude the provision of these services on site, it is important that they are available nearby or on schedule with the project phasing. These services and facilities may include schools, parks, shopping centers, recreation facilities, and emergency services such as fire stations and medical clinics. Ascertaining if these services are available is also important for the ZLL concept when clustering is used to provide open space and recreation facilities. In this case, it would be most economical not to duplicate services already available, but to concentrate on other facilities or pass the savings on to the consumer. Again, regulations should not call for common facilities already provided beyond the financial ability of the project or those not needed by the future residents.

Economic Considerations

While there are a number of physical and cultural aspects of any site that must be identified and analyzed, it is essential that the revenues, expenses, and profit of the development for each potential site be identified as well. Prior to or during the option stage of the purchase of land, numerous cash flow studies and rate of return analyses should be prepared to have a better understanding of the implications of site, utility service, market, and development costs for that particular parcel. Sufficient data should be generated from the first phase site analysis and market analysis to allow a "ball park" financial evaluation. That evaluation should be a cash flow which responds to the time value of money. Based on the cash flow, the internal rate of return can be estimated, thereby allowing the developer to compare alternative investments, revise his development plan and program, or seek other sites. Too many sites are purchased without these financial studies, thereby leading to reduced profits, losses, or bankruptcy.

The fact that the project being analyzed is a ZLL one does not alter the fundamental approach to the financial analysis. What is unique to the project is that there may be (but does not necessarily have to be) some unusual cost elements when compared to standard single-family development, where little may be done to improve on the project quality. Fencing and walls will typically occur more frequently in a ZLL project; landscape treatment, particularly in model

homes, may be more extensive in order that the concept of total lot usage can be better presented to the buyer; and streetscape design and amenity packages must be thoroughly planned and may exceed typical expenditures.

Essential elements to the "before purchase" cash flow are:

- The estimated absorption rate of the lots or units to be built
- Sales prices for these products
- The land release terms for the purchase of the parcel
- The conceptual land plan
- The "hard and soft" development costs for the project.

Each of these elements should be kept at the broad level of detail, which has tended to be more accurate than trying to desegregate each element into its many components. Particularly in the area of development costs, an estimate of overall costs per acre or per lot of development would be better than estimating the exact linear feet of all the various utility lines and road sections that may be built within the project.

One issue which must be considered, since it affects the go/no-go decision on the project, are the off-site utility costs for water, sewer, and power. More than just the overall cost of the off-site utilities must be identified; other considerations are who pays for the improvements, what are the financing alternatives, and how will the payments be made. In many areas off-site utilities can be handled through special district taxation as opposed to front-end expenses for the developer. Another question that should be answered is, "Are there any interim systems or phasing of systems that can be adopted to lower the front-end costs for the development?"

Prior to bringing a project to reality, it is recommended that steps be taken to protect the future consumer to insure that policies for off-site costs are fair and equitable. Adjacent peripheral roads not serving the project and policies on rebates for service extensions are two good examples.

It is generally recognized that the cost of doing a proper amount of homework is much less than the cost of purchasing the wrong site, or the right site at the wrong price. These preliminary tests of the cash flow of a proposed project are intended to give ball park evaluations of the profitability of the project, and are not intended to be the conclusive financial and cash flow studies for the development. Much more detailed cash flows should be prepared after the master plan has been finalized, after the units, amenities, and marketing programs have been spelled out in detail, and while the project is being built.

3-12 and 3-13 Landscape expenditures, particularly in model homes or sales centers, may be higher than standard. These expenditures are important in terms of demonstrating to homebuyers the potential uses of the courtyards and entries on ZLL homes.

4 Basic Development Considerations

A ZLL project is usually undertaken as a response to certain needs:

- To develop better and more competitive residential environments in all price ranges
- To gain density and reduce costs
- To make a small house and its lot more attractive
- To make higher land values work while providing detached units
- To meet specialized market demand in some regions for a compact single-family house (For example, many empty nester market segments might be attracted to a ZLL project.)
- To maximize lot usability and reduce outside maintenance
- To make more efficient use of individual lots.

4-1 The higher densities of ZLL development require innovative lot layout and street design.

Each aspect of the land plan and building program should be evaluated for reinforcement of the ZLL concept. There needs to be interaction among the various disciplines, such as planning, architecture, access, drainage, etc., that may not be critical in conventional single-family residential subdivision development but is very critical in ZLL. For instance, placing large houses close together on small lots may have negative selling impacts unless the design and layout compensates through architectural treatment, building placement, or abundant landscaping. The lot size and configuration may be affected by the size and design of models as well as by building or fire codes. Therefore, before too much design is done, planners should check with regulatory agencies. There are often complications for anything other than the single-family lot developments. Finally, long, narrow walled-in yards may make yard drainage complicated, requiring a civil engineer to be involved in conception of the house/lot layout.

If a pioneering effort is being made in ZLL development, some real soul-searching must be made. There must be definitive reasons to support ZLL development, such as better environment, more saleable product, added density, or lower costs. Assuming a developer/builder is experienced in single-family subdivisions, the ZLL concept is the logical transition to achieving higher densities without significantly changing markets. There must be an awareness of market acceptability; many single-family submarkets can be identified. ZLL can and does provide a better project than many conventional ones.

In many communities, the other big hurdle is obtaining public agency approvals for the ZLL project. Older zoning ordinances and subdivision regulations, where standard setbacks are required, will require modifications or variances in order to develop ZLL. Some communities will want to use their cluster or planned development zone district. (See the ordinance included in Appendix B for reference.) Unfortunately, most communities do not have a standard zone that will allow ZLL concepts, and time is wasted passing new ordinances, applying for variances, and using the PUD or similar ordinances. ZLL is not a major departure and standard zones should allow it as a use by right, or new zones should be set.

4-2 This square cul-de-sac provides an opportunity to arrange the garages and dwellings in an interesting pattern. Vegetation softens the impact of solid building facades.

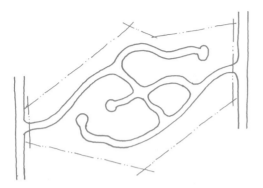

ATTEMPT TO CREATE TOO
MUCH "VARIETY" FOR VISUAL
INTEREST

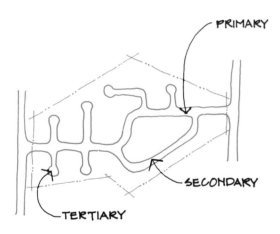

PRIMARY

SECONDARY

TERTIARY

MORE LOGICAL STREET PATTERN
TO USERS/VISITORS

4-3 A hierarchy of streets and a logical layout are essential. Too much variety in street
alignment causes confusion.

Streets

Auto access should be a key development consideration. Circulation for vehicles is usually required at each dwelling unit. A hierarchy of streets should be established, based on traffic flow patterns. The fewer the number of houses on a street, the narrower it can be and not interrupt traffic movement. This subject has been addressed by many planners, usually to the effect that public requirements for street widths are normally excessive and out of scale and based upon speed performance rather than need. Private streets are sometimes the solution, in which case a homeowners' association must be prepared to assume the maintenance costs, but private streets are not an appropriate solution. If the governing agency allows streets narrower than subdivision regulations provide for, without jeopardy to the health, safety, and welfare of future residents, they should be public. Unfortunately, we are slow to change and to accept better ideas that are more economical and balanced for user needs. Residents on private streets pay twice for maintenance.

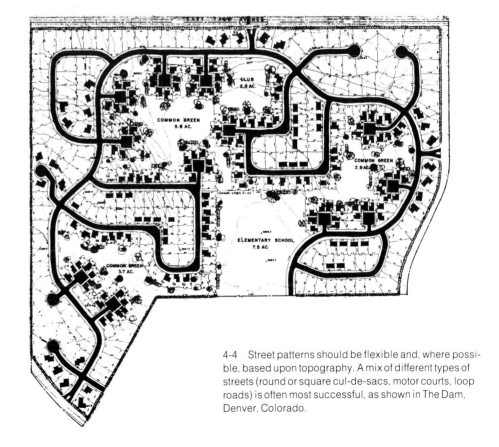

4-4 Street patterns should be flexible and, where possible, based upon topography. A mix of different types of
streets (round or square cul-de-sacs, motor courts, loop
roads) is often most successful, as shown in The Dam,
Denver, Colorado.

Street patterns should be flexible and based upon the topography, the need for efficiency, interest, the project concept, and costs. Cul-de-sacs and loops on curvilinear streets are both acceptable. Public acceptance appears to rest on the interest created or lack of interest. With small lots, it is easy for the long streets to be monotonous and uninteresting. While streets should be the shortest possible, lengths should be based upon the need for efficient lotting. Shorter street lengths tend to "lose" lots but appear well worth the increased design interest and, therefore, saleability.

Consideration should be given to placing ZLL programs on loops and cul-de-sacs and leaving collector roads devoid of lots. The increased yield in density on loop and cul-de-sacs plus a narrower collector road (lower cost, no driveways, no on-street parking, more efficient traffic flow) should sufficiently trade off for land losses in this design approach. Comparisons of cost should be made. The highest densities are not neces-

4-5 and 4-6 The narrower frontages in ZLL can create monotonous streetscenes if long, straight streets are used. Interest and variation can be created through the use of cul-de-sacs and shorter streets.

4-7 In choosing street treatment, care must be taken to not allow streets to become too wide or too dominant. This street in the village of Woodbridge shows an excellent blend of a narrower street and effective planting.

sarily the most saleable and, therefore, most profitable.

Minimizing lot widths is a big factor in getting efficient ratios of street and utility length per lot. Making the dwelling as narrow as possible toward the street should be a goal in the floor plan design. Market acceptance more than interior functioning will be the major constraint. As mentioned earlier, street width and length is often the place for economizing on capital improvements; however, length has a more direct application to long-term efficient circulation.

Efficient circulation patterns are the most important aspect of energy conservation in considering a ZLL development. While a circuitous pattern can provide privacy and elimination of through traffic, it should be balanced against efficient circulation, addressing, and identity. Each one-quarter mile extra that must be traveled may mean hundreds of extra miles each year for vehicle access to the dwelling.

When determining the layout and design criteria for a circulation system for the ZLL project, consider the following:

- For local traffic conditions, 20- to 24-foot streets are often adequate, assuming a parking pad in front of each garage or carport. Many publications, such as Residential Streets by ULI/ASCE/NAHB, offer logic in sizing streets. Consider providing guest parking in bays when streets get as narrow as 20 feet. Two to four parking bays per unit should be sufficient when considering that most multifamily projects require one and one-half to two parking stalls per unit. Limited rare street congestion on special occasions may not be justification for excessive street standards.
- Common private drives serving several dwellings can work, depending on parking solutions.
- The view from the street is important in creating an inviting neighborhood

atmosphere. Alignment of the street itself contributes to this.

- Curving or broken alignments to prevent long views down the street are usually preferable to grid street patterns or long straight streets. In a well thought out plan, street alignments can be designed to be interesting as well as to accomplish other siting objectives, such as appropriate topography and existing tree cover.
- Logical addressing and continuity should not be sacrificed in an attempt to provide too much variety, as is sometimes the case with "creative" land plans.
- The probability aspects of floodplains should be applied when setting street standards for fire access, police access, and others.
The probability of two cars meeting on a loop or cul-de-sac is low enough to warrant consideration of one moving lane.

- Standard street designs which allow for on-street parking require going to and from homes through "linear parking lots." Cities should re-examine on-street parking requirements.
- Narrower streets cause traffic to slow down. This, plus eliminating on-street parking, can make ZLL projects safer.
- Narrower streets are "in scale" with narrower lots and houses. Wide streets are "out of scale" and reduce the visual quality and saleability of the ZLL concept.

Organization of a street image achieving the above objectives is usually more difficult for ZLL than with conventional single-family subdivisions because of the minimal width lots. Garage doors or carports become more dominant, often occupying half or more of the building width. With good design these become very acceptable. Facade treatments are one solution. Site planning solutions can provide more complete assurances that too

4-10 and 4-11 Narrow streets and lots can still permit necessary access for emergency vehicles, moving vans, and garbage trucks without allowing the street to become the dominant feature.

4-8 and 4-9 In most residential developments, and especially in ZLL developments, narrow streets can exist without interrupting traffic movement. Sidewalks are generally unnecessary and elimination of curbs and gutters can provide a pleasing setting.

4-12 Curvilinear streets can add variety to an otherwise long, straight view. This is especially important for ZLL developments.

many garage doors are not visable from one location. Pavement texture of driveways can assist. For instance, a series of cul-de-sacs off an internal collector which has no houses fronting on it will present garages to the viewer only when he enters the specific cul-de-sac. The internal collector streetscape would display only the sides of housing and fencing. Through clustering and ZLL concepts it is possible to put all homes on loops or cul-de-sacs as the most desirable arrangement.

Street detailing is important to a project. Items such as sensitively designed curbing (or no curbing, just valley gutters) and mailbox posts add interest and distinction to the streetscape. Pavement texture and color can add quality to cul-de-sac ends. Landscaping is usually the key to softening ZLL density projects to where the proximity of structures does not overwhelm the observer. This often happens in new projects that do not include street-side landscaping with the purchase price.

Standard street designs normally are not acceptable. There is currently a trend toward basing street design on other values than speed and service, such as user needs. In some instances, curbs can be dropped, allowing drainage to recharge groundwater supplies and lessen costs for storm drainage.

4-13 Collector streets normally do not have units fronting on them. This area can be utilized as a landscaped strip, enhancing the community.

4-14 and 4-15 Site design, facade treatment, and landscaping can help produce pleasing streetscapes. In ZLL developments garages become prominent and care must be taken to avoid a monotonous streetscene.

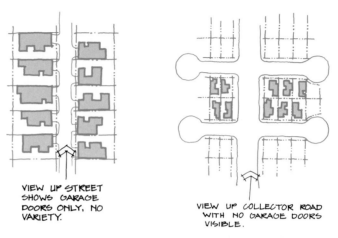

VIEW UP STREET SHOWS GARAGE DOORS ONLY, NO VARIETY.

VIEW UP COLLECTOR ROAD WITH NO GARAGE DOORS VISIBLE.

4-16 and 4-17 Having too many garage doors in view should be avoided. Shorter streets and varied unit type and setback can help.

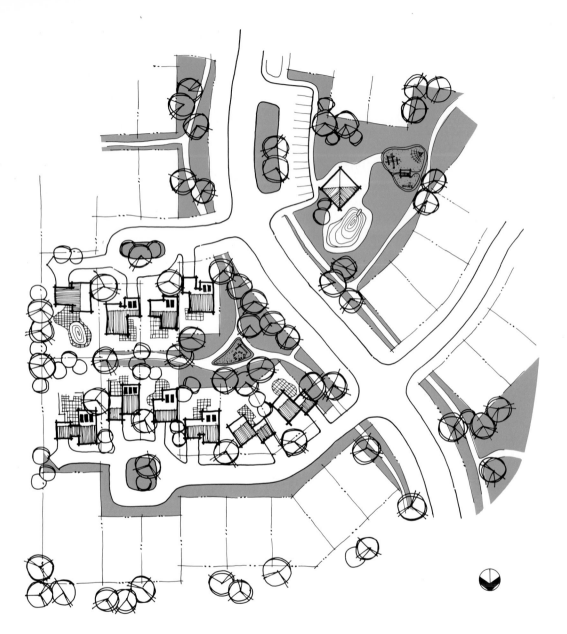

4-18   Large, centrally located open spaces are more
valuable than numerous small landscaped strips.

Open Space and Recreation

The normally higher density of a ZLL project can require that attention be paid to open areas for visual relief, recreation, and exercise. The open space can be an integral part of the project design and correspond with the marketing profile and user needs. Not all projects have to have open space; sometimes a nearby public park provides an ideal open space recreation function. Also, in shelter markets, open areas are more difficult to justify from the standpoint of costs, depending upon the price level.

A tendency in the past has been to provide more open space than was warranted. While it made planning sense and a good marketing package initially, it put a financial burden on the homeowners who had to maintain and operate it after the planner and developer were finished. Recently, the idea that each project needs a clubhouse and swimming pool has been re-evaluated. Similarly, open space is being used less extravagantly than in the early PUDs, where common open space was located behind each lot. Larger open areas are more valuable than several 20- to 50-foot bands of open space throughout the project. A single, larger open space, strategically placed within the project, can have many advantages. Maintenance costs per acre are considered low compared to strip linkages. The cost/benefit is considered greater.

If consistent with the project's lifestyle, large open areas can be made into public parks so there will be less maintenance burden on the homeowners. Projects with private parks require residents to pay double for park and recreation maintenance and development. Obviously, private, exclusive projects would not want the open space publicly dedicated. For lower cost projects, however, it may be the only viable way to provide for it. If communities require open space and recreation facilities as part of the approval process, then such facilities should be public at the option of the developer or residents.

Homeowner association fee "lowballing," whereby the developer subsidizes maintenance and operational costs in the early years to help support the amenity package, is not recommended. It is not until the developer leaves the project that the homeowners often discover the actual cost of operating the amenity package. The '80s should see a more realistic approach to amenity packages. Construction prices have been rising, making the common ownership of a swimming pool more of a luxury to include in the sales package, for instance. Recreation needs should be carefully assessed. Use of recreation facilities as a sales tool has been done extensively in the past; it is questionable if it will remain a good idea.

4-19 "Pocket" parks containing play equipment, picnic facilities, and opportunities for sun and shade are less expensive to maintain, provide relief from the higher densities, and attract children and adults alike.

4-20 and 4-21 Narrow rear lot open space connections often are unused or underutilized. Fences separate the space from the homeowner and become costly maintenance items.

Maximum use of open areas on the lot itself should be planned in the ZLL project. If done properly, the space can be every bit as useful as a conventional single-family yard. (Indeed, many question the usefulness of single-family yards!) Quality of the space compensates for quantity, especially in certain "lifestyle" developments. Outdoor areas on the lot should be planned for use accessibility. Will the side yard be used to garden, used as a deck and pool area, be a mowed lawn area, be a dog run, or be used to park a camper? All have their place, depending on target submarkets.

The primary determining factors leading to a decision to include common open space or recreational amenities in a potential ZLL project will be the balance between the development costs for the amenities and the enhanced market appeal of the ZLL complex. The following seven factors will all be instrumental in determining the amenity package for a specific ZLL development.

Political Requirements. Depending on specific political jurisdiction, one may have fairly rigid requirements on the land area and improvements to be devoted to amenities. As mentioned earlier, amenities, if any,

should be based on project objectives, resident needs, and cost concerns.

Location. Since many ZLL developments are on infill sites, they may be in proximity to an existing park or recreation center. Duplication of existing public amenities would seem unnecessary unless the element of private amenities could be a meaningful sales tool.

Site Features. Steep slopes, floodplains, and ponds or lakes can be utilized very effectively in the form of common open space, allowing overall density equal to or greater than conventional single-family lotting and the simultaneous preservation of natural amenities.

Target Market. The age, income, and family status of the target market will strongly influence the amenity package. Thorough market research will lead to identification of the more appealing amenities for that market group.

Cost. The target price range of units, relative to development costs, will determine the availability of funds for amenity development.

4-22 and 4-23 Open space should be consolidated into usable areas rather than narrow isolated strips. Large areas such as parks should be located in such a manner as to provide visual relief from the road. Landscaped strips should be large enough to be usable.

Maintenance. It may be necessary to dedicate the recreational amenities to the city or, for political, homeowner cost, and marketing reasons, it may be wise to avoid establishing a homeowner association for maintaining the development amenities. In that case there will probably be definite limits on what the jurisdiction will accept for public maintenance. In any case, a builder/developer will want to be sensitive to the ultimate homeowner obligation for maintenance. Small or narrow strips cost more to develop and maintain. Collecting small areas into larger areas can cost less and have greater community benefit.

Competition. Probably the most significant determinant of all is the level, type, and quality of amenities provided by competitors in the market. Even if it is the first ZLL development in a city, the project will be competing against other residential developments of all types for buyers. A careful determination of the product/price equation (including recreational amenities) relative to the competition must be made.

The matrices on the following page relate typical recreational amenities to various life-cycle groups and also to typical land requirements and costs.

4-25 The amenities provided in The Crossings can be a marketing tool, when geared to the target market.

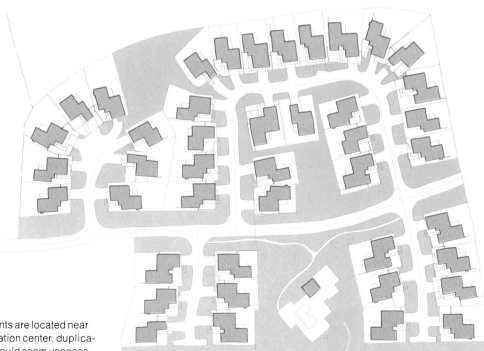

-24 If ZLL developments are located near existing park or recreation center, duplication of these amenities would seem unnecessary unless private amenities are to be used s a sales tool.

45

Recreational Amenities

| | Life-Cycle Compatibility | | | | | | | |
| | Families With Children | | | | | | | |
	Young Singles	Young Couples	Pre-School	Pre-Teens	Teen Agers	Empty Nesters	Active Retired	Retired
Walking/Jogging Path	*	*	*	0	0	0	0	—
Open Space /Natural Areas	—	—	0	*	*	0	—	—
Sitting Areas	—	—	—	—	—	0	*	*
Picnic Area	—	*	*	*	—	—	—	—
Tennis Courts	*	*	*	0	*	—	—	—
Paddle Tennis Courts	0	*	0	0	0	0	—	—
Racketball Courts	*	*	*	*	0	—	—	—
Swimming Pool	*	*	0	0	0	0	0	—
Clubhouse	*	0	—	—	—	0	0	—
Weight Room	0	0	—	—	—	—	—	—
Field Game Area	—	—	—	*	*	—	—	—
Tot Lot	—	—	*	—	—	—	—	—
Golf Course	—	—	0	*	*	*	*	—
Par 3 Course	—	0	0	*	*	*	—	—
Putting Green	—	—	—	*	*	*	*	—
Basketball Court	0	0	—	*	—	—	—	*
Horse Shoes	—	—	—	—	—	*	*	*
Lawn Bowling (Boccie)	—	—	—	—	—	0	*	*
Shuffleboard	—	—	—	0	—	—	*	*
Pond/Lake	0	0	0	*	*	0	0	0
Sailing	—	0	—	*	*	0	—	—
Horse Facilities	—	—	—	—	—	—	—	—

* Strong Compatibility,   0 Moderate Compatibility,   — Low Compatibility

Recreational Amenities

	Land Requirement	Development Cost	Maintenance Cost
Walking/Jogging Path	Variable	Moderate	Low
Open Space/Natural Areas	Variable	Low	Low
Sitting Areas	.1 – .25 acre	Low	Low
Picnic Area	.5 – 1 acre	Low	Low
Tennis Courts	.5 acre/2 courts	Moderate	Moderate
Paddle Tennis Courts	32'x60' for 2 courts	Moderate	Moderate
Racketball Courts	60'x45' for 2 courts	High	Moderate
Swimming Pool	2 acres	High	High
Clubhouse	1 acre with parking	High	High
Weight Room	Part of clubhouse	Moderate (with clubhouse)	Moderate
Field Game Area	2–3 acres	Moderate	Moderate
Tot Lot	.5 acre per lot	Moderate	Moderate
Golf Course	120 acres for 18 holes	High	High
Par 3 Course	60 acres for 18 holes	High	High
Putting Green	.25 acre	Moderate	Moderate
Basketball Court	60'x100' on parking lot	Moderate	Low
Horse Shoes	12'x40' for 1 run	Low	Low
Lawn Bowling (Boccie)	30'x80' for field	Low	Low
Shuffleboard	10'x64' for field	Moderate	Low
Pond/Lake	Variable	Depends on site	Low
Sailing	.25 acre for dock, etc.	High	High
Horse Facilities	2–5 acres for stable, etc.	High	Usually Leased

4-26 In all developments, the location of major recreational features or amenities is very important. It can be either centrally located, at the "front door" of the project, or dispersed at several locations throughout the development.

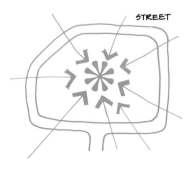

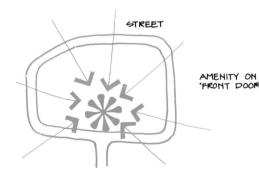

When recreational amenities do occur, they can be placed at a project's front door for immediate sales appeal, be central to the project (equal distance from the people it serves), or be dispersed throughout the project. Not any one method is superior to another in every instance but rather is a function of the individual program. Generally, a desire for a strong social magnet leads one to consider a centrally located unified complex; however, spatial constraints or more specialized groupings oriented to a given amenity call for dispersed facilities. Marketing considerations, when placed above livability of the project, dictate a "front door" location. However, depending upon the configuration of the parcel, the "front door" and central locations can often be one and the same.

Effective utilization of land, increased density, and maintenance considerations have produced a trend toward grouping open spaces in large consolidated areas. This eliminates the "strip" open spaces which have usually provided a certain amount of openness to the land plan. The feeling of openness in projects has become very important as the number of units per acre in cluster subdivisions has increased from three to four. Some planners also thought that it was necessary due to the closeness of houses. This still may be so in some areas; however, it is now necessary to re-examine current amenity requirements due to rising costs, the need for energy conservation, the difficulty homeowners have in paying high cost maintenance for facilities that are not being fully utilized, and the knowledge of how to design small lot projects without a lot of wasted open space. Where valid, amenities should be included; where not, and where good project design occurs, they should be omitted.

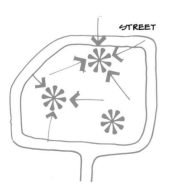

STREET

AMENITIES DISPERSED

4-27 Amenities can be provided in a variety of forms. Open space along the entry road to Country Walk sets the feeling for a target market. 4-28 and 4-29 Play equipment for children should be sturdy to withstand years of use.

Environment and Image

Overall impressions of a development are formed on how well the design team was able to integrate the streets, dwellings, and open spaces into the desired setting. Visual interest and appeal should be a goal of all housing, even in the basic shelter market. The ZLL project generally deserves more such attention than conventional single-family housing because the lot size stigma needs to be overcome. Landscaping, again, is the most common cure. A small space can be as appealing as a larger one depending on the quality of treatment.

Successive chapters on site design, architecture, landscaping, and amenities cover each subject in detail, but the following suggestions are made for visually organizing a ZLL project.

- The buyer generally selects the area of town in which to live, the project edge and entry, the project, the street image (from the model area, earlier phases), and, then if the home meets basic needs, the house.
- The perimeter of the project area which borders on streets can be landscaped or fenced in a continuous manner. The treatment does not need to be on common open space, but if it is on private property, some uniform maintenance will be required for it to remain effective.
- An identity sign or complete program of signage should be designed to coordinate with the project name and character.
- Upon entering the project area, views from the streets toward open space can lessen the impact of density.

- Visual impressions from within the dwelling should, again, be ones planned to expand space.

Size of project is possibly more important than density in establishing an identity. ZLL projects from 100 to 150 dwellings, or from 15 to 40 acres, generally fall within limits of a desirable marketing/phasing package and are manageable from the visual identity standpoint. The large tracts of a third- to a quarter-acre single-family lots, the standard by which suburban development is judged, are the ZLL competition. This was not always the case. Remember Levittown and its overwhelming scale after World War II? If the ZLL product becomes the standard, as it is in many regions (such as Southern California), then perhaps scale of projects will become less important.

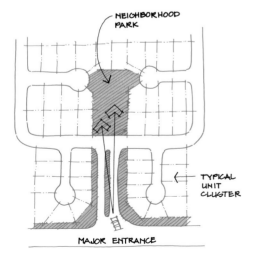

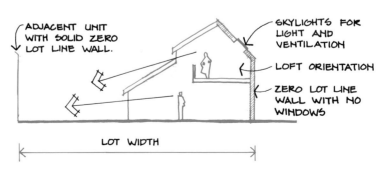

4-30 Careful consideration should be given to the viewers' first impression. As a person enters the development, open park areas strategically planned can offer visual interest.

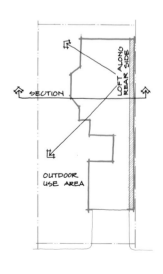

4-31 Views from within the unit should be directed outside to create a feeling of larger space. Wherever possible, second-story windows should be located in such a manner as to prevent views into adjacent courtyards.

Energy Conservation Techniques

Lot siting is the single most important factor setting up the house/lot combination for long-term energy conservation. Regional climatic responses, of course, dictate orientation. Usually it is desirable to promote solar gain in winter and block it in summer. Planning streets to channel cooling summer breezes or to avoid channelizing winter winds may also be possible. Wind scoops directed into building interiors have been used for years in certain climates. The ZLL house, being directional to one side of the lot, makes siting consideration more important than in conventional single-family housing. The dwelling can be either very sunny or very cold. The ZLL house, with the blank wall generally to the north and the big side yard generally to the south, makes a natural passive solar configuration. Project boundaries, small projects, and the need for higher densities and cost reduction may outweigh energy orientation aspects where achieving such would be a conflict.

4-32 Even rooms such as the bedroom can be opened up to the outside with large windows and gardens. The back wall of a garden area may be the garage of the adjacent unit.

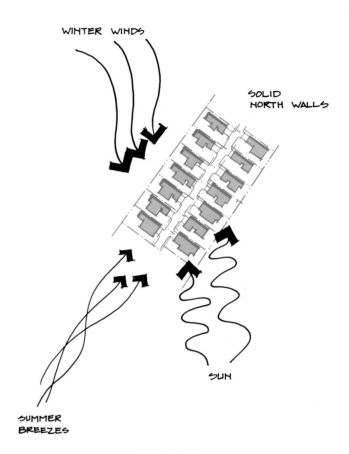

4-33 The ZLL house, with the blank wall generally to the north and the side yard generally to the south, makes a natural, passive solar configuration.

4-34 Careful attention needs to be given to the land plan regarding bulk so that the adjacent unit is not shadowed. In addition to the roof, the wall of the adjacent unit also can be utilized for passive or active solar techniques.

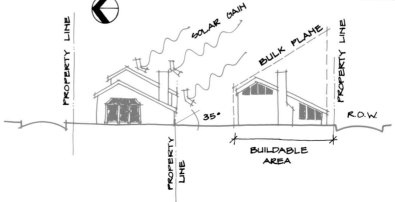

Solar Access Rights

The project can be planned to assure optimum climatic access, depending on density and building heights. In the 1980s, such considerations will be very important to most developments. Most financial institutions require permanent legal access rights to sun sources if the dwelling is designed for active or passive solar functions. Permanent access requires that trees will not intrude into the three-dimensional solar envelope. Careful attention needs to be given to the land plan regarding building bulk and the landscape plan regarding size of mature plants. As discussed later, solar access easements are now a part of some community zoning ordinances.

Building Arrangements

The primary feature of a ZLL home which distinguishes it from a conventional home is that the structure is seemingly turned "sideways" on the lot. This is due to the narrowness of the typical ZLL lot. It should be noted that this is not necessarily always the situation, since zero lot line concepts may be applied to more conventionally sized lots of 50- to 60-foot widths.

Unless other conditions exist, the garage dominates the streetscene in most ZLL projects. Care should be taken to soften the impact and create more interest through the use of landscape materials and arrangement of ground cover. Entry to the home is through a court or small yard located along one lot line. Depending upon setbacks, very interesting gates or archways can distinguish this area. All living areas have physical or visual access to a variety of sitting courts or small activity areas (outdoor rooms). Often

the rear fence is "transparent" to allow visual access to the common area, but it can be solid where privacy is important. Bedrooms can have visual access to the common area and streetscene. Attention needs to be given to the privacy of outdoor use areas. Many programs use one-story structures. Others predominate with two-story types.

Building relationships can be rectilinear in nature or sited orthogonally at cul-de-sacs. This rectilinear organization is recommended for two reasons: (1) density and land efficiency is maximized and (2) architectural relationships are improved. Where space allows, streets and open space should be allowed to "meander" in an effort to create interest and reduce a "grid" approach; clusters of buildings should be set at an angle whenever possible for the same reason.

4-35   In this two-story unit, the yard opens up to rear open space and the main floor rooms face outside. This unit arrangement can work with or without rear open space.   4-36   In the single-story unit, bedrooms face rear open space and living rooms face interior courts.   4-37 Two-story unit with rear entry.

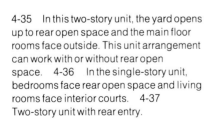

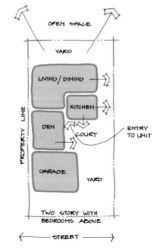

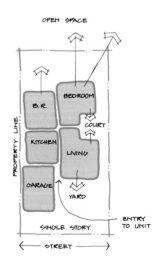

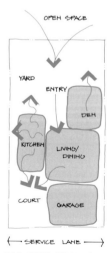

The trend to smaller front yard setbacks has seen a need for improved treatment of this space. In many cases greater architectural treatment with walls and hard surfaces requiring low maintenance is used. However, a trend to improve landscape treatment is also prevalent with emphasis needed on more "lush" landscape materials, organized into pleasant compositions, and greater attention to quality finished details. Each treatment needs to be balanced to the pricing goals.

The important issue here is that large setbacks do not necessarily mean an improved streetscene. However, a poorly treated smaller setback can impact negatively on sales. Attention needs to be given to producing a high quality streetscene to remove the buyer's attention from large or small homes placed on small lots close together. The viewer should be drawn to the landscape, architectural, or detail aspects.

CONVENTIONAL SITING
EFFECTIVENESS IS
LESSENED AS DENSITY
INCREASES.

ORTHOGONAL
SITING

4-38   Conventional and orthogonal siting.

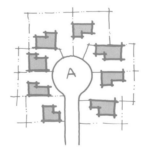

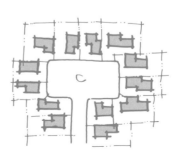

4-39   Cluster options utilizing orthogonal siting: A utilizes a conventional cul-de-sac; B utilizes a square cul-de-sac; C expands the square cul-de-sac into a motor court; and D is a double square cul-de-sac.

Installation of Utilities

Generally, single-family lot practices for distribution of infrastructure are applicable to the ZLL concept. Sewer and water lines are usually located in the street in front of the units, while electric, phone, CATV, and other cables are laid underground in the rear lot easement. Higher density ZLL projects, however, may dictate that all utilities be on the street side. The rear yard is narrow and possibly obscured with privacy fences so that it may become more practical to place even electric and phone lines in front. Placement of meters, junction boxes, transformer boxes, and similar hardware becomes very important.

Water Efficiency

The ZLL concept itself does not have direct implications on water usage. However, with side yards being more fully developed as use areas and with less emphasis on large front and rear yards, it becomes evident that traditional single-family lot landscaping concepts should be modified to fit ZLL situations. In many areas of the U.S. today, water is becoming more precious, and residential lots that have efficiently irrigated landscapes are timely. The ZLL lot, by size alone, should reduce irrigation water use demands over regular single-family lots. Plant and landscape materials can further reduce water consumption.

Amenity programs as part of a ZLL development should likewise carefully evaluate the amount of water used. Lakes, streams, and water features and the landscape development should be planned with maintenance and operating costs in mind.

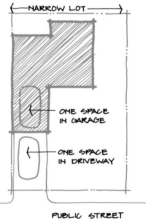

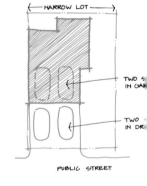

4-40, 4-41, and 4-42 Parking spaces per unit: single-car garage, one space in driveway; two-car garage, two spaces in driveway; two-car garage, two spaces in driveway and two street spaces.

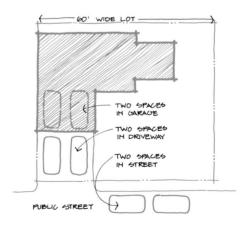

Parking

Parking requirements obviously vary from project to project depending upon the type of occupant toward which the project is oriented. Age, lifestyle, regional location, and project relation to adjacent areas can all vary the parking requirements.

Minimum parking requirements should be two to two-and-one-half spaces per dwelling unit. Normal layouts provide either two or four spaces on each lot with additional spaces on the street. It is not uncommon to have as many as six parking spaces per unit provided in the final design although this is not necessary. Most communities need to update their regulations for parking for single-family housing to be more consistent with national goals for energy conservation, lower cost housing, and parking regulations for multifamily projects.

The provision of garage parking is not always necessary. Some regional locations do not require garages; some programs require an alternative to a garage—either a carport, a stall, or a combination of the two. The absence of a garage usually allows more lot area to be put into the living areas, either interior or exterior. Garages, when provided, may be sized as small as 18 feet by 20 feet for smaller cars.

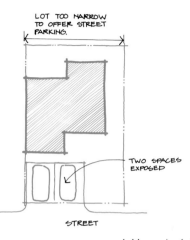

4-44 and 4-45 Garage, street parking, and carports are all viable alternatives.

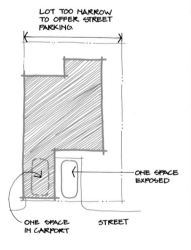

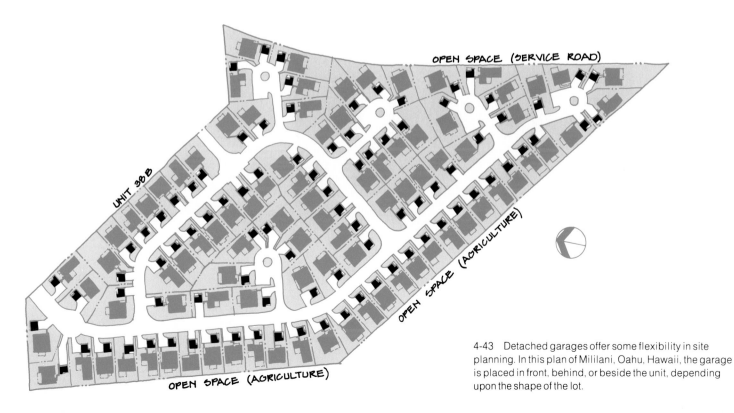

4-43 Detached garages offer some flexibility in site planning. In this plan of Mililani, Oahu, Hawaii, the garage is placed in front, behind, or beside the unit, depending upon the shape of the lot.

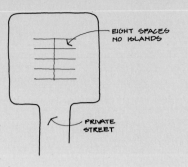
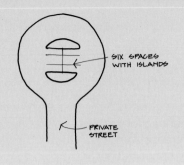

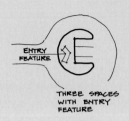

EIGHT SPACES NO ISLANDS

PRIVATE STREET

SIX SPACES WITH ISLANDS

PRIVATE STREET

SIX ANGLED SPACES WITH ISLANDS

ENTRY FEATURE

THREE SPACES WITH ENTRY FEATURE

4-46 Cul-de-sac and parking variations.

Driveway parking, if provided, should allow a distance of at least 18 feet from the inside edge of the sidewalk to the garage door. Driveways of five to 18 feet long should be avoided because, if they are used for parking, the vehicle may extend across the sidewalk or into the street, interfering with pedestrians or traffic flow. Overflow parking may be accommodated on the street, especially if public streets are utilized. However, when a project has private streets, alternate methods of providing for overflow parking can be incorporated if deemed necessary. One alternative is to provide for an island in the center of the cul-de-sac. Several design variations are possible. Another alternative

4-47, 4-48, 4-49, and 4-50 Parking alternatives and varied driveway lengths; (4-47) driveway just long enough to accommodate a car length; (4-48) garage with side access allows for two cars on the lot, with minimal garage setback; (4-49) again, minimal garage setback but with off-street parking for guests; and (4-50) driveway lengths of five to 18 feet should be avoided to discourage parking across the sidewalk and into the street.

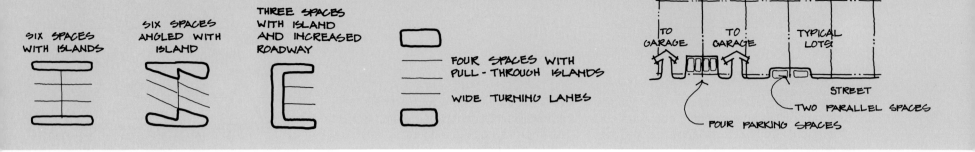

SIX SPACES
WITH ISLANDS

SIX SPACES
ANGLED WITH
ISLAND

THREE SPACES
WITH ISLAND
AND INCREASED
ROADWAY

FOUR SPACES WITH
PULL-THROUGH ISLANDS

WIDE TURNING LANES

PROPERTY LINES

TO
GARAGE

TO
GARAGE

TYPICAL
LOTS

STREET

TWO PARALLEL SPACES

FOUR PARKING SPACES

is to provide spaces either in parallel or right angle configurations. When these considerations are not desired, some other location can be provided, possibly removed from the cluster, but still within easy walking distance of 250 to 500 feet.

Very often, however, the need for overflow parking is overemphasized for the few times it is needed versus its cost. The need for overflow parking should be studied and provided if, and only if, the user needs are being met. Some projects may not need as much as others, and some may need none at all. Parking should be based upon consumer needs on a project-by-project basis and not as an across-the-board requirement.

4-51 and 4-52 Guest parking in motor courts can be handled in several ways. Trees and textured paving mark the stalls at Caswell Court. (4-52) Circular tree wells mark the area for guest parking at Whetstone.

Pedestrian Access

Pedestrian access from each home to a destination point is an element of changing considerations. Early ZLL concepts backed, or fronted, each individual lot on a common area. This is still true today of many programs with lower densities. However, increased density requires that many lotting configurations eliminate common areas adjacent to each lot, thereby requiring more traditional use of front door walk areas.

Access from each lot to a destination point can be either from the front or rear. Traditionally, front access connects with a sidewalk, though trends would indicate less sidewalks in recent well-planned projects. As improved design occurs, on-street parking is eliminated or minimized and as more loop and cul-de-sac designs occur (with few lots on collectors or other busy streets), pedestrian traffic can use pavement edges or the grass. Sidewalks can be used on one side of the street. Tot lots can be conveniently placed to encourage their use. As concrete is a high cost, high energy user, sidewalks should be minimized. Past importance of sidewalks may have been over-empha-

4-53 Open space can be provided as common area at the rear of lots. Care must be taken, however, to assure that open space of this kind does not become a maintenance burden on the homeowners.

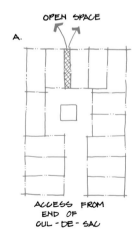

OPEN SPACE

A.

ACCESS FROM END OF CUL-DE-SAC

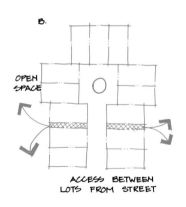

B.

OPEN SPACE

ACCESS BETWEEN LOTS FROM STREET

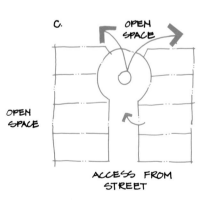

C.

OPEN SPACE

OPEN SPACE

ACCESS FROM STREET

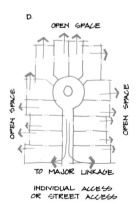

D.

OPEN SPACE

OPEN SPACE

OPEN SPACE

TO MAJOR LINKAGE

INDIVIDUAL ACCESS OR STREET ACCESS

4-54 Pedestrian access from each lot to open space can occur from the front, utilizing sidewalks and easements, or from the rear of the lot. A and B utilize easements between lots, C utilizes a cul-de-sac opening up onto open space, and D utilizes rear lot access and major open space linkage.

sized. Rear access, when occurring, can connect to a trail in the common area.

When cul-de-sacs or roads are extended to "touch" an open space area, pedestrian access can conveniently link to the paved area. Properly designed cul-de-sacs, and often the entire vehicular system when designed to slow and discourage traffic, can be very acceptable for pedestrian traffic, especially if on-street parking is removed and thus the potential safety hazard of children moving out between autos is removed.

4-56, 4-57, and 4-58 Open space with pedestrian walkways provides linkage within the project.

5 Market Considerations

In any significant land development, market analysis plays a key role in setting guidelines for the character, scope, and timing of a project. ZLL development is no exception, and since it is a relatively new housing product in most communities, market analysis will be vital to such a project.

For ZLL developments, as for other types of housing, two basic markets exist: the shelter market in which ZLL units comprise the lowest priced single-family detached housing available and the specialty or lifestyle market, where prices are comparable to competitive housing types and the chief attraction is the distinction of having security, low maintenance, unique design, and possibly increased recreational opportunities.

5-1 Common areas that provide playgrounds and picnic areas can serve as excellent marketing tools, besides being a desirable amenity within the project.

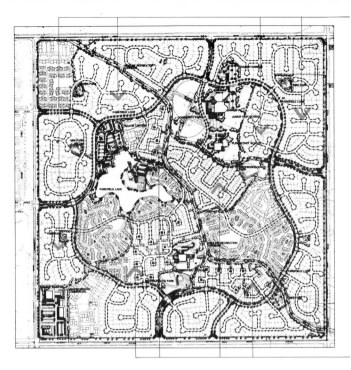

• STRONGLY
RECOMMENDED
ZERO LOT LINE
UNITS.

• OPTIONAL ON ALL
SINGLE FAMILY LOTS-
MODIFICATION OF
ZERO LOT LINE
RECOMMENDED.

• DEFINITELY ZERO
LOT LINE UNITS

5-2 Depending upon the market analysis, some parcels within a project should be developed as zero lot line while others should be set up to be either zero lot line or conventional, depending upon market trends.

The shelter market is often comprised of individuals, young couples, and families who would consider the ZLL unit as a starter house. These families have simply been priced out of the conventional "large lot" detached single-family home. The primary buying objective of this group is to find shelter in a detached unit and to get into the ownership housing value increase escalator. Increasingly, multifamily units are meeting this objective due to price constraints. ZLL homes become a short-term means of being able to afford the "ultimate" home. In contrast, the specialty market looks at its housing unit as an end, the best unit to fulfill their lifestyle at present and in the near future. Almost everyone today is concerned about the strong appreciation potential of home

ZERO LOT LINE MARKETS		
	SHELTER MARKET	**SPECIALTY MARKET**
CONCEPT	• Starter House—lowest priced detached unit, probably a "temporary" home	• Lifestyle preference over other equal or lower priced units—lower maintenance, higher security, and common amenities
TYPICAL MARKET	• Low- to middle-income singles and young families	• Middle- to upper-income professionals, empty nesters, retirees, etc.
TYPICAL DENSITIES	• 5-9 units per acre	• 3-8 units per acre
DEVELOPMENT FEATURES	• An affordable detached unit—usually avoiding open space, homeowners' associations, etc.	• Quality lifestyle units, with common theme/amenities (lake, tennis, etc.)
MARKETING CONCERNS	• Reassurance about value appreciation potentials	• A better product for the target market than competitors
DESIGN CONCERNS	• Minimization of building mass impacts on project appeal—maximum facade, detailing, and landscaping—with limited budget	• Proper mix of lot sizes, unit sizes, features, common amenities, and development image for maximum appeal to target market

59

ownership. In fact, the appreciation potential of a smaller, more energy efficient unit at a desirable location can be a major marketing plus for ZLL housing.

Specialty housing can appeal to a number of different groups, such as young individuals or couples, empty nesters, retirees, etc. While still providing a detached unit lot available for the owners' use ZLL housing also provides relatively low maintenance requirements, potentially higher security, and privacy. Also, specialty developments are often built around a recreational element,

such as tennis, golf course, or other open space amenities.

There are major differences in the market and marketing/sales approach for the shelter and specialty markets. ZLL housing in shelter markets can range up to five to nine units per acre, with relatively few amenities in the development. Most likely, there will not be a major investment in common open space or recreational amenities. In the lifestyle market, the density would generally be lower, probably ranging from three to eight units per acre, frequently with more investment in

open space amenities. It should be noted that density is not as important as how well the project is designed and finished. Final appearance is a major key to success.

Observing housing and socioeconomic trends in the United States and Canada indicates that ZLL housing, particularly in the shelter market, should become more predominant in future years. As major segments of the housing market are priced out of the conventional single-family detached home, ZLL becomes the most economically accessible detached housing alternative.

5-3   Much can be done to alleviate buyer apprehension over the ZLL concept by giving special attention to landscaping details in the model homes.

Market Acceptance of ZLL Housing

There are, at present, three identifiable stages of ZLL housing acceptance in various markets. Stage 1 consists primarily of smaller markets where there has been virtually no experience with this housing concept. Stage 2 cities, such as Denver and Chicago, have had a fair amount of experience with ZLL housing, but it still represents a relatively small portion (perhaps 10 to 20 percent) of total new housing production and a very small percentage of total housing stock. Stage 3 markets include Southern California and selected markets in Florida (i.e. metropolitan Miami) where ZLL housing now represents a major component of total new housing construction (40 to 50 percent) and is considered standard.

The problems of determining the target market and market potential are different for each situation. A further distinction is made between the low end shelter market and the higher priced lifestyle housing market.

The major concern in a Stage 1 market is to determine when sufficient potential exists for the first or second ZLL development in the community. The key objective of the market analysis, therefore, is to determine whether a significant share of potential homebuyers have been priced out of the conventional housing market or whether a substantial lifestyle market segment is not being adequately served. Concurrently, research should evaluate buyer attitudes and determine the level of public awareness of ZLL housing, thereby aiding the structure of the marketing program. Since ZLL is ideal for infill sites, this initial analysis should include the availability of close-in housing.

The questions concerning Stage 2 markets include what the total amount of available demand is, where new desirable locational opportunities are, and whether all of the potential submarket groups for ZLL housing are being adequately served.

In both Stage 1 and 2 markets the lack of buyer experience and a fear of the unknown are important considerations. Unless properly designed, landscaped, and marketed, these problems can be compounded by an unsatisfactory appearance of ZLL housing. Therefore, the developer of early ZLL complexes in any market must produce a superior product and still accept the fact that his marketing effort will be largely educational, acquainting people with the benefits and easing their apprehensions about this concept.

There are fewer variables to assess in Stage 3 markets, since the initial buyer apprehension over ZLL housing has largely been overcome. In Southern California, for example, ZLL housing is rapidly becoming the standard for most new detached single-family housing purchases. This includes all of the middle- and upper-income groups, virtually all age groups, and households with and without children.

5-4 Unit entries in ZLL can have special significance to the homebuyer. They must provide a private, individual welcome.

Buyer Profile and Motivations

There are three valid sources of information to assist in market decisions:

- Market Research—this is needed to document the market segments, competitive housing, changing demand factors, and other elements relative to the market.
- Comparable Developments—the actual experience of other similar developments in the local or other markets can also be quite useful. The market analysis could collect information from these developments. Direct builder to builder contact might also be beneficial.
- Developer Intuition—when used in combination with other market research techniques, this can be a valuable tool. This is particularly true with innovative products.

Because the market for ZLL housing is relatively new and is experiencing fairly rapid changes in almost every part of the country, the following discussion cannot be a prescription for a particular market. It is intended as a guide and presents certain experience to date.

A builder/developer, in evaluating the feasibility of using a professional market research firm, should consider both local and national firms. If ZLL housing is new to the area, the advantages of a consultant with actual experience with innovative housing products will probably outweigh a lack of familiarity with the local market. The developer should meet with representatives of two to three firms, providing as much information as possible about his experience, market, budget, and plans. It is usually more productive to provide all consultants with a reasonable budget level and then to compare their experience, qualifications, proposed approach, and products. By forcing a competitive bidding situation, the developer will have a more difficult time making price/quality comparisons.

A traditional market analysis uses market information available from planning departments, chambers of commerce, population and housing censuses, interviews, surveys of competition, etc., to determine market potential. Market studies, regardless of the complexity or type of uses involved, should include the following eight elements:

General Economic Background. This element sets the perspective for the entire analysis and development through an assessment of recent and anticipated trends in the local economy. At this point, answers

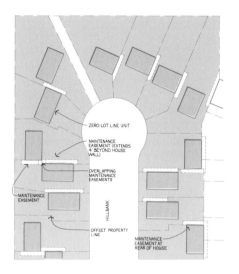

ZERO LOT LINE UNIT

MAINTENANCE EASEMENT (EXTENDS 4' BEYOND HOUSE WALL)

OVERLAPPING MAINTENANCE EASEMENTS

MAINTENANCE EASEMENT

HILLBANK

OFFSET PROPERTY LINE

MAINTENANCE EASEMENT AT REAR OF HOUSE

5-5   Buyer profile and market analysis are very important to the success of a zero lot line project. Central Park, located in the new town of Bramalea, northwest of Toronto, Canada, was a testing ground for zero lot line techniques. This project utilizes many nonstandard techniques such as variable lot shapes, minimum setbacks, alternative parking, and specialized easements.

5-6   View down Hillbank Street, Central Park. Notice that there are no sidewalks and no curbs.

are found for such questions as who are the major employers, what kinds of future cycles can be anticipated in those industries, and is information available concerning specific expansion or contraction plans. The result of this research should be a forecast of future employment opportunities, population, and the number of households in the market. A profile of the population by age, income, occupation, and household size should also be created.

Site Analysis. While the old maxim of "location, location, location" still holds true, this does not cover which aspects of site location are most important. The factors to assess include recent market momentum in terms of desirable growth vectors versus slower growth areas. Other important factors include access, compatibility of surrounding uses, proximity to targeted market, exposure, the nature of recent and anticipated new developments in the site area, and the general public image of the location.

Where ZLL developments are not the norm, it is strongly advised that new developments not vary from the established direction of development. While there are exceptions, the attempt to combine a new concept with a secondary location will result in slow market acceptance or even failure. The challenges of selling a new concept will be strong even without the added complication of attracting customers to a secondary location. Fortunately, ZLL developments are ideal for infill sites, so strong site opportunities probably exist even in more developed areas.

Assessment of Competition. This can be the most revealing step in the entire market analysis process. It can also be, because of the difficulty in obtaining information, the most frustrating.

Visits should be made to as many competitive residential developments in the subject community as possible. Identifications of marketing programs, product, features, price, rate of absorption, and profile of recent buyers should be completed. Consider what these projects are doing right in terms of development design and marketing program, as well as what they are doing wrong. It is also important to meet with the local planning and zoning administrations to identify their reactions to these developments and to identify any proposed developments.

Insight and experience can be gained by visiting comparable developments and talking with both the sales staff and the developer. From the sales staff, information can be obtained about marketing approaches and levels of appeal to various market segments. From the developer, his experience in political processes, financing difficulties, and other important elements of successful development will be beneficial.

Historic Trends. Overall trends regarding housing development in the subject community should be reviewed. From the detailed information already obtained, a profile of lot sizes, unit sizes, and prices for the past several years can be established.

Market Area Definition. The first component of market definition is the geographic trade area for the subject site. This area could be the entire community, or in the case of a larger metropolitan area, a subsector of that metropolis. Important elements to consider are the location of major employment centers, the accessibility to the site, generally recognized barriers (major highways, railroads, etc.), and typical employment commuting times for the community. The second component is the market segment that is the target of the proposed development. For example, if targeted toward young professional couples, identify the location of major professional employment centers and major entertainment districts. If targeted toward traditional families, closer attention should be paid to school district boundaries.

Market Projections. Once the geographic trade area and functional market segments are defined, it is necessary to develop projections for that market which will tell the size of the total market within which the project will be competing. Here again, information from local planning studies of population and housing, as well as information from the population and housing censuses, are suitable resources.

Generally, projections beyond three to five years are virtually meaningless; two-year projections are most useful. Adjustments to the projections can be made based upon subjective data, such as the impact of new industry relocations to the area.

CURRENT RESIDENTIAL INVENTORY

	Unit Type	Unit Price	Unit Sq. Ft.	Lot Dimensions	Starting Date	Total Units Sold	Total Units Planned	Absorportion Per Month	Projected Completion
1. Southbridge/U.S. Homes	S.F. Within 1 yr. T.H. Cluster	Southbridge I $75.000- $87.000 Southbridge II $130.000- $150.000	1.140- 2.653	Vary	May 1980	Phase I 30 Phase II 13	1.500	6	1983
2. Oakbrook/Medema	S.F.	$ 85.750- $ 93.950	1.513- 2.236	75x100	1978	200	400	11 (average)	April 1982
3. Woodridge/Wood Bros.	S.F.	$ 87.000- $ 97.000	1.850- 2.350	minimum 7.200	1977	300	400	10	—
4. Glenn Oaks	Condo	$ 42.000		—			205		
5. Southglenn Commons	Condos (some leased)	$ 39.500- $ 65.500	808- 1.355	—	Jan. 1980	80	240	10	Spring 1981
6. Tiffany/Nu-West	S.F.	$121.000- $145.000	2.400- 2.893	minimum 70x110	March 1979	49	71	3	December 1980
7. Hidden Hills (7.5 acres)	T.H.	$ 87.000- $ 93.000	1.270- 1.565	—	April 1980	25	72	5–6	June 1981
8. Heritage Greens/Celebrity	S.F.	$112.000- $165.000	1.900- 2.600	80x110	Nov. 1979	110	500	10	1985
9. Chaumont in Baumont/ Cherry Hills Investments	S.F. (custom)	$ 89.500- $140.000	—	½ acre or 1 acre	1979	12	54	—	—

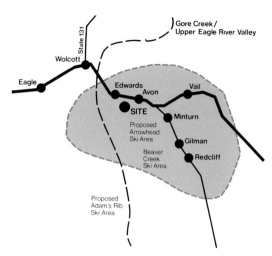

5-7 An example of market area definition in a rural area.

Potential Site Share. At this stage the assessment of competition should be used as the basis to estimate potential site share for the trade area and market segment of the total market potential. The proposed development should be weighed against various competitors in terms of relative strengths and weaknesses. Subsequently, estimates of the existing market share of competitors and estimates of the share which could realistically be achieved by the subject development should be made.

Site Development Potential. Finally, combining all of the previously developed information together, it is possible to estimate the market potential for the site. If justified, some additional support may be added which will come from beyond the specific trade area (the additional support should not exceed more than 15 to 20 percent of the total potential). At this point, the development plan for the project should be defined. The target markets should be evident, and suitable housing products, densities, and price ranges should be identified.

1980–1990 HOUSING UNIT DEMAND

County	1980 Housing Stock[1]	1990 Housing Demand[2]	New Households	1980–1990 Demand Replacement[3]	Total	Average Annual Demand
Adams	90,103	122,200	32,100	4,500	36,600	3,700
Arapahoe	111,679	184,000	72,300	5,600	77,900	7,800
Boulder	75,421	94,200	18,800	3,800	22,600	2,300
Denver	227,521	253,100	25,600	11,400	37,000	3,700
Douglas	8,732	23,300	14,600	400	15,000	1,500
Gilpin	1,448	900	—	100	100	100
Jefferson	138,884	180,000	41,100	6,900	48,000	4,800
SMSA TOTAL	653,788	857,700	204,500	32,700	237,200	23,800

[1] 1980 housing start from the Provisional Census of Population and Housing for 1980.
[2] Housing demand is based on projected households and a 5 percent vacancy rate.
[3] Replacement demand is calculated at 0.5 percent per year.

EMPLOYMENT, POPULATION, AND HOUSEHOLD FORECASTS

	Employment	Employment Participation	Population	Average Household Size	Households
1970–80 Average Annual Increase	33,500		33,700		21,900
Percent	5.1%		2.4%		4.5%
1977–80 Average Annual Increase	46,100		31,100		25,100
Percent	6.1%		2.1%		4.5%
1980	856,500	54.3%	1,576,576	2.57	613,984
1980–1990 Average Annual Increase	40,400		42,200		20,100
Percent	3.9%		2.4%		2.9%
1990	1,260,700	63.1%	1,998,600	2.45	814,800
1990–2000 Average Annual Increase	43,400		51,000		49,300
Percent	3.0%		2.3%		
2000	1,695,100	67.6%	2,508,900	2.42	1,037,400

65

Consumer Surveys

There are several limitations of traditional market research particularly when applied to new products such as ZLL housing. Market research normally looks backward to see what has occurred in the past. This approach is understandable and useful, but it can cause missed opportunities, as well as carry major risks (i.e., by the time data is collected, processed, and published, it is out of date). In the evaluation of broad income, life-cycle groups, there is a major gulf between the available information and its specific meaning and needs for a development. Quantitative data may be useless. Buyer perceptions of and reactions to the ZLL concept are the critical questions to be answered in the market research.

Consumer surveys, buyer profiles, and focus groups will provide the quantitative information needed to design the ZLL project. Once the general character of a target market group has been identified, the buyer profile can aid in defining needs, desires, and motivations. Research and/or professional assistance is highly desirable in order to insure a truly representative sample and to avoid biasing the questions and results. (A little information can truly be dangerous if it is not accurate.)

There are a number of questions which need to be answered before designing the survey program, such as:

- How much time is available for the research?
- How many target markets are there, and how big are they?
- How broad is the range of information to be covered?
- How great does the detail need to be (degree of accuracy wanted)?
- How big is the research budget?
- Who will interpret the results?

Then, the specific method of research (telephone survey, model home questionnaire, mail survey, door-to-door survey in a target residential area, focus groups, etc.) will need to be established. The method of selection of the sample and the issue/question approach will need to be defined. Both land planning and architectural questions should be included in order to better "tune" the design to the potential buyers. Finally, the interpretation and application of results will need to be completed at the conclusion of the study.

There is virtually no limit to the range of issues which can be studied and utilized in concept planning and design. Therefore, an important element of the process is to focus on a realistic range of data targeted in the buyer profile. Some interesting issues include the following:

Profile.

- Age, income, occupation, household size
- Number and age of children
- Work patterns, location of work, and commuting patterns
- Hobbies and recreational interests (cooking, gardening, reading, day sailing, etc.)
- Recreation vehicle (boat, motorcycle) ownership
- Number and type of pets

Image.

- Color preferences
- Texture reactions
- Name response
- Life pattern (interests, hobbies, time spent at home, entertaining patterns, etc.)
- Reactions to geographic areas
- Amount of entertaining (dinner, weekend, etc.) per year and attendance
- Importance and preference of facades

Development Features.

- Location and image
- Amenities
- Level of control
- Homeowners' association
- Bigger yards vs. smaller yards with common areas and features
- Importance of walking distance to schools
- Response to narrow streets
- Importance of off-street parking
- Level of resistance to occasional party parking congestion
- Like/dislike of yard work

Unit Features.

- Number of bedrooms
- Number of bathrooms
- Elevation
- Floor pattern
- Storage space and location
- Garage size (one, two, or three cars)
- Basement
- Room arrangements (ranch, split, two-story)
- Pricing
- Price structure (standard vs. optional features)
- Outside activities desired on the lot

The approach should be designed carefully. For example, graphics and sketches can be extremely useful in properly communicating concepts, in opening up discussion, and in testing ideas. This is particularly true in dealing with new concepts where examples may not be available in the area.

The use of focus groups has proved to be very productive in generating qualitative information. A focus group is a small group of people that are personally interviewed by a trained attitudinal researcher. The group is selected from members of the target market and usually paid a fee for participating in the interview. The researcher will follow a carefully prepared set of questions designed to gain answers to very detailed questions.

Research can be extremely useful in responding to questions of new product design in order to develop innovations with lower risk factors, as well as for answering "what-if" and tradeoff questions. With proper design and implementation, this research can carry through the entire planning, architectural design, and marketing program for a development. It will also assist in designing for the needs and interests of the consumer instead of designs based on assumptions, competitive products, or upon sometimes antiquated standards or regulations that affect land development.

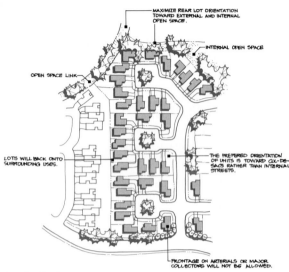

MAXIMIZE REAR LOT ORIENTATION
TOWARD EXTERNAL AND INTERNAL
OPEN SPACE.

INTERNAL OPEN SPACE

OPEN SPACE LINK

LOTS WILL BACK ONTO
SURROUNDING USES.

THE PREFERED ORIENTATION
OF UNITS IS TOWARD CUL-DE-
SACS RATHER THAN INTERNAL
STREETS.

FRONTAGE ON ARTERIALS OR MAJOR
COLLECTORS WILL NOT BE ALLOWED.

Layout and Design
Single Family Cluster

5-8 When laying out a zero lot line development, orientation of units is one of the most critical factors.

Design Considerations

Several of the more important design considerations include:

Location. In markets where ZLL housing is not the norm, the location is extremely important. The site should be in a strong growth area for the market segment being attracted, with as many as possible amenities such as parks, restaurants, and shopping nearby. It is important not to combine a new concept with a secondary location. Fortunately, since ZLL development is ideal for infill sites, good locations in desirable areas should be available.

Size of Development. It is desirable to develop enough units to create an overall community image while keeping the development small enough to permit flexibility. A useful rule of thumb would be to develop a six-month phase; that is, plan for enough units at a time to supply six months of demand (as projected in your market analysis).

There are a number of reasons not to develop too large a complex, particularly in a new market. The first is the evolving nature of ZLL housing. That is, the developer will be learning more about ZLL developments as he builds, and so will the target market. Desirable range for early ZLL developments in a market is generally between 60 to 250 units. This will permit the use of infill sites to create a single image and movement to a new site with a second generation design. Another advantage of this size project, particularly where there will not be open common space included in the development, is that the high density of the development will not overwhelm prospective buyers with too much mass. And finally, should the market response and absorption be short of the builder's goal, he will be able to easily "shift gears" into a different housing product or price.

Flexibility. This is not a specific design feature, but should be considered in all development planning. As much flexibility as possible should be included for periodically changing unit densities, project features, and price levels as the market evolves.

Design Details. Unit and site design details should be planned with input from the qualitative studies of the market. These details will vary by target market; therefore, no one unit design can meet the needs of all markets. Variety is essential.

Model Treatment. The landscaping of front and back yards in model homes needs as much careful attention as does the interior decoration of the units. In ZLL housing, the yard is seen as an extension of the unit. Therefore, the yard landscaping needs to be keyed to the prospective buyer use profile. For example, young families with infants will need lawns and play areas, while professional couples may require more formal landscaping with decks and hot tubs. Model units assist sales through displaying the ZLL range of ideas and maximum uses of the smaller yards.

Amenities and Finish. The type and quantity of amenities, as well as the level of finish in the units, is totally dependent on the price range targeted for the development, consumer interest, and availability within the project environs. In higher-end developments, extensive open space and amenities may be necessary. In the lower priced shelter market, cost will probably be the primary concern.

5-9 Model home areas are particularly important in ZLL. Besides selling a single-family home, the developer is selling a concept and particular attention must be paid to site, street, and building design.

5-10 Fencing, signage, and parking are important considerations when laying out a model home complex. Landscaping demonstrates to the owner the potential look and use of their outdoor spaces, and the fencing and signage help direct the potential buyer through the homes display.

5-11 ZLL development can be accomplished in all prices ranges. Trails Village in Chicago is a moderately priced project. 5-12 A home in Misty Cove on Hilton Head Island, a second home community.

Market Range. Lot size is not an indication of house price. Additional "on-lot" amenities may serve the medium to luxury markets. These amenities might include exterior hot tubs, pools, fountains, private bedroom courts, decks, trellises, and landscaping; interior amenities could include master bedroom suites possibly with whirlpool tubs, upgraded kitchens, additional bathrooms, and more exciting spaces. Luxury, low, and moderate priced units can be designed for the buyers who want the advantages of single-family living but who do not care to maintain the typical luxury single-family residence and grounds.

Proximity to Existing Development. If targeted to a similar market, there are several advantages to locating a ZLL development in proximity to a more conventional project. This will generate buyer traffic, allow for a more direct comparison of features and prices, and permit flexibility in the number of units developed.

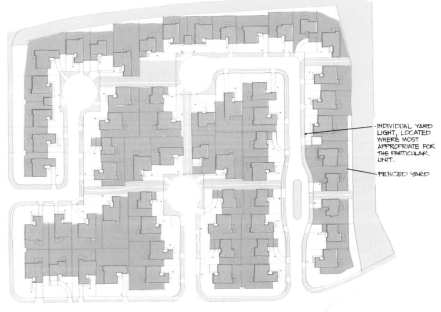

INDIVIDUAL YARD LIGHT, LOCATED WHERE MOST APPROPRIATE FOR THE PARTICULAR UNIT.

FENCED YARD

5-13 Phelps Luck in Columbia, Maryland, utilizes very little open space. Each backyard is fenced and each unit has its own yard light.

Traffic and Buyer Feedback. It is also important to use questionnaires and follow-up interviews with buyers of the units. This information will allow the appeal of your ZLL development to be improved. In addition, it helps to build referral business for future units. It is extremely difficult to obtain accurate data from shopper traffic and, therefore, such surveys would normally be avoided. Shopper traffic will probably not represent a sample of the community nor of the purchasers. In addition, much of the traffic consists of recreational shoppers who are not really in the market. Therefore, a survey of this group will not normally yield useful product or marketing data. Under normal circumstances it will be more useful to deal with a selected sample group or with actual purchasers.

Financial Considerations. It may be necessary to exert some extra effort to obtain financing for a ZLL development in a new market. Any problems, however, can be reduced or eliminated based on the track record of the builder and careful preparation of the financial application package. Specifically, the following steps will be of assistance in obtaining financing:

- It would be helpful to complete a thorough research and consumer survey program and document the research and findings. A complete, well-organized report should be prepared for presentation.
- It may also be extremely useful to prepare case studies of successful ZLL developments in other markets for the banker. Include information concerning price, size, rate of sales, market appeal, as well as photographs and site plans of these developments in order to compare with the proposed program.
- It is also useful to talk to the financing sources for those developments, and, if appropriate, furnish contact names and telephone numbers to the banker. Reassurance from his peers concerning the viability of the concept should help reduce concerns over a new program in your community.

6 Building Design

Critical to the success of any ZLL project is the sensitive design of the various housing units. Rarely can a single-family or townhouse plan be modified to actually achieve the advantages and concepts of ZLL housing. While houses are usually unsuccessful when transported from another region or project, if the developer has had particularly good success with a certain ZLL unit and desires to use it for another project it may be modified to meet the new site conditions, consumer profile, orientation, climate, architectural theme, and market criteria of the new site. The important point is to plan the housing units specifically for each individual project.

6-1 Building design is especially important in higher density ZLL developments to provide interest and variety.

Control of the design on large projects may be accomplished by a design review committee appointed by the developer. Authority of the committee as well as parameters of design should be clearly and completely written into the land sales documents. The approval of the committee should be a requirement for building permits. Parameters of design should not be overly limiting, but should generally include:

- Architectural design style
- Color
- Roofing materials
- Streetscape considerations
- Fencing materials and heights
- Landscaping.

The designers should be allowed adequate freedom to produce fresh, innovative units. While a lack of parameters may permit bad designs, design review committees should be oriented to a process that assures improved design rather than administering "you can" and "you can't" stipulations.

6-2   The sensitive design of the various housing units and their layout is critical to ZLL project success. Notice the numerous patios, both side and rear, of these homes at Green Run in Virginia.

Unit Types

In the ZLL concept of housing, all the standard floor plans, such as single-story, two-story, split level—all with or without basements—may be used. Hopefully, with more emphasis placed on ZLL housing, innovative, clever variations of floor plans will surface to create more interesting and energy efficient units that are appealing to the mass market.

Each unit type has opportunities which should be analyzed along with market research to produce the best unit for a particular consumer market. In a single-story unit, privacy is probably more easily accom-

plished than in a two-story unit, as second-story windows allow views into neighboring yards. Two-story structures tend to predominate for projects with smaller lots (4,000 square feet or so). This results in narrower and shallower lots; a narrow, deep lot with a narrow deep home can provide another alternative. Also, single-story units have larger footprints than comparably sized two-story units and, therefore, use up more land area—a critical problem on a small lot. Split level units may be designed to use less land area than a one-story unit by, in effect, creating a two-story unit partially depressed into the ground. Such units may also be used to

create necessary grade change on lots requiring heavy contouring. Basements can be included in all units to increase storage, utility, and indoor recreation spaces in areas where basements are needed and accepted, either by buyer preference or acceptable soil and subsurface water conditions. A mix of single-story, split level, and two-story units will probably produce an interesting and marketable total project. In any event, units to be used on small lots usually require more thought and sensitivity in design to create the maximum livability, privacy, and economy inherent in ZLL housing.

UPPER LEVEL

Lot Line Wall Design

Limitless exciting floor plans can be created with the given restrictions of a ZLL wall and the anticipated consumer. This wall (or walls) becomes a very useful design tool by serving as an anchor wall for the particular unit as well as a privacy screen for the adjoining unit. The lot line wall can be a side lot line wall, rear lot line wall, or a combination of either. The front lot line wall may also be utilized with no restrictions on window or door openings. While designing the units for a given project, siting of the units should be kept in mind in order to avoid attached housing by abutting lot line walls of adjoining units, unless this is a design option. Typically, a project should contain a variety of units which, when sited, will avoid this problem.

Lot lines can also be laid out to follow building walls so that an irregularly shaped lot could be created. The solid wall of the lot line can serve as a great wind buffer if that is desirable in the particular geographical area. Cold winter north or west winds in the northern climates can be buffered by the solid wall placed on north or west lot lines.

The desirability of shading from the sun or encouraging "capture" of cooling summer winds in the southern climates may dictate other locations.

A linear floor plan stretched along the lot line may create more of a perimeter wall than a conventional compact house and therefore this type unit may be more costly per square foot. However, the total living environment and saleability should be considered and promoted rather than simply the dollar cost. Of great advantage for a linear design in cold climates is the tremendous passive solar gain which can be collected with the proper building orientation.

Some climates allow a great deal of glassed area in the wall facing the on-the-line wall. This lets the space of the room "leak out," seem larger, and allow the outside to "come in." Architectural and artistic treatment of this bare wall can be diverse. Permanent designs can be attached or provisions for some additions or hangings can occur through deed restriction.

6-3 Floor plans for four zero lot line units, Pheasant Run, Greeley, Colorado. Note the use of an atrium.

6-4 and 6-5 Applicable building codes should be investigated early in the design process, focusing particularly on the lot line walls. At Approach '80, an experimental housing tract in Las Vegas, Nevada, the same unit, one with a garage and one without, has differing requirements depending upon size and location of adjacent units. The unit in 6-4 does not require a parapet wall for fire rating safety but the same unit in 6-5 was required to have a parapet wall, due to the size of the adjacent unit.

Building Code Considerations

Early in the design process, applicable building codes should be investigated. Most codes have not specifically addressed the ZLL concept. Fire ratings for walls are still determined by proximity to a lot line rather than distance between buildings, though the latter is gaining acceptance. Therefore, if PUD restrictions can supercede local building codes, the documents should be so written that lot line walls need not be fire rated. Rather, fire rated wall requirements should be determined by distance between buildings. Typically, a residential wall within three feet of a lot line is required by most codes to be one-hour fire rated. Therefore, if separation between walls of adjoining units is more than six feet, fire ratings should not be necessary, regardless of the property line boundaries.

The PUD covenants and guidelines should specifically address this problem so that fire rated walls are not required and owners are not penalized by codes which have not been updated to include the ZLL concept. Where possible, change should be made in ex-

isting building codes to accommodate ZLL concepts. Otherwise, the owner is penalized because a frame fire rated wall costs more to build than a nonrated frame exterior wall, since the exterior stud must be protected on both sides by fire rated gypsum board as opposed to no gypsum board requirements on a nonrated wall.

Siting of units also should take into consideration access for fire fighting. The smaller lots create a concentration of building structures often with very small yards and passageways, which is a consideration for emergency access not too different from townhomes.

Typically, building codes do not allow openings (windows or doors) in walls situated on a lot line. This restriction hardly penalizes the design of a unit, however, since low windows or doors are not desirable on lot line walls in ZLL units. Higher windows for light and ventilation may be desirable and building code changes should be sought to allow this.

Building codes also restrict roof overhangs, cornices, and gutters in a variety of ways with respect to lot line walls. These restrictions may create very real design problems and should be addressed in the PUD documents. Check the applicable codes for such restrictions. Provisions can be made for overhangs in deed restrictions, covenants, or easements when necessary.

If the PUD documents (or other applicable zoning) cannot be structured to avoid these building code problems, or if the project is not to be classed a PUD, variance to the code should be requested from local jurisdictions in order to create an acceptable and economical ZLL project. In many cities, the building code cannot be superceded by PUD or other zoning requirements. Accordingly, the developer must request variances if the local codes are too restrictive or will cause additional unnecessary expenditures. Perhaps as more ZLL projects are designed and more variances are requested, codes will be updated and restructured to recognize the concepts of ZLL housing.

Solar Considerations

When designing units, siting the units to take advantage of solar energy should be kept in mind. Large glass areas with poor orientation should be avoided. Figure 6-6 shows a well-planned two-story unit which would orient well on an east or west facing lot so that the large glass areas of the living and dining rooms would face east or south (in some climes, to the west). This unit would not, however, site very well on a lot situated on the north side of the street in a cold climate, though it may not be avoided. The large glass area would then face north and eliminate the possibility of any solar gain. Generally, all units site well on lots facing a north-south street as the lot line wall can be situated on the north lot line in cold climates and the south lot line in warm climates, allowing for the proper window orientation toward or away from the sun. Lots facing on an east-west street require specially designed units to allow for proper orientation of glass areas with respect to the sun. Whatever the orientation, the architectural design can be oriented to enhance solar considerations.

6-6   When designing units, the actual siting should be kept in mind to avoid large glass areas with poor orientation. This unit utilizes south and east sunlight in its window placement.

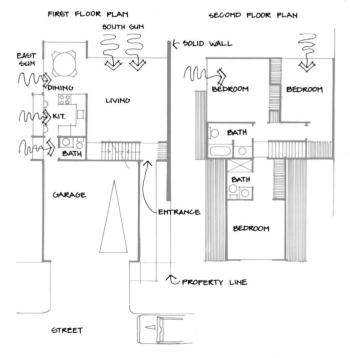

Architectural Theme

Any project, ZLL or not, should be conceived with an integrating architectural theme or style. The theme should be one which is sensitive to the local market and one with which the developer, through his marketing team, feels comfortable. Architectural styles vary from the traditional historic and regional styles to crisp contemporary. French farm house or chateau, Italian villa, English half timber, and Spanish stucco describe certain historic styles, while New England salt box, New Orleans wrought iron, Midwest farm house, and California mission describe regional styles of architecture. Continuity in the style of all buildings within a project, including housing units, club houses, sales buildings, and entrance gates, creates a sense of community or neighborhood. Within a large project, the continuity of theme or style can be varied to avoid monotony by using divisions within the style, as for instance, New England salt box, Boston townhouse, Nantucket seaport—all of which are variations of the New England theme. While style and theme are very personal preferences, the choice should be somewhat sympathetic to the climate, region, and user preferences. Many styles will look natural, for instance, in the sunny warm climates of the country. It is wise to concentrate on the styles compatible with the established regional style rather than import an absolutely foreign style.

6-7, 6-8, and 6-9 ZLL can be adopted to a variety of architectural styles.

Building Materials and Colors

The ZLL concept of housing invites the use of any of the building materials common to single-family construction. The budget for the unit will dictate the range of materials, along with local tradition and buyer preference. Materials from unit to unit should not vary widely as the streetscape quickly becomes cluttered and confusing. Continuity of materials can be made interesting by varying the colors and textures; for example, all siding on units may be chosen as plywood for purposes of cost. Wood battens can be placed over plywood vertically on certain units and stained. Rough sawn or smooth faced plywood can be used on adjoining units with stain of another, but harmonious, color. Still another color may be introduced for the wood trim. However, each of the colors chosen for a given streetscape should be compatible and blend with all the other colors on that given street. This avoids the confused look seen so often. Brick and stone can create beautiful accents if used well. On small lots with the units built close together and close to the street, the use of materials and colors which create a light feeling, such as light colored stucco or light colored bricks, is much more desirable than the use of heavy red or dark brick or oppressive dark wood colors. The dark colors create good accents but can create a grim, enclosing streetscape, especially before the lawns and plantings mature to soften and partially obscure the building surfaces. Climate should be also considered when choosing colors. The long grey winters in the northern climates can be cheered up with brighter colors if chosen well, while the hot sunny climates require more subdued colors.

6-10, 6-11, and 6-12 A variety of colors and textures, depending upon the developer's budget, can be used to enhance aesthetic appeal.

Roofs

As previously mentioned, streetscapes can be rather grim until the trees and shrubbery mature to soften the precise, crisp building surfaces of the units, and the grass in the parkways grows and adds colorful relief to the gray concrete, black paving, and soil. (Many buyers are turned off or on during this stage of construction.) During the period while the landscaping matures, the roofs are particularly prominent. Color and materials should be carefully chosen. Wood shake and wood shingle roofs certainly create interesting beautiful surfaces and add continuity to a complete project. Roof colors and materials are often the same for continuity. Clay tile roofs add equal interest and continuity but, unfortunately, all projects cannot afford the cost. Asphalt shingles create a good durable roof and pleasing effects can be accomplished with stock colors.

When choosing colors for a complete project, it is a good idea to choose perhaps three colors at the very most with little color variation between the three. Though not a pat solution, projects with a lot of color variation help make up for uninteresting architecture. For example, a tan, light brown, and medium brown or similar shades of gray create desirable aesthetics in some projects. Heavy colors such as black, dark brown, or deep green become oppressive in large quantities and should be avoided.

Roofs should be interesting in shape as well as color and texture. Long sweeping roof lines can be very interesting and beautiful with proper material choice and color. Roofs with many hips, valleys, gables, and ridges can become costly and tedious and create a very cluttered streetscape. Shed roofs lend themselves well to the ZLL design concept.

Roof designs should also consider watersheds and stormwater collection points. While runoff must be a consideration in overall design, it need not necessarily limit roof designs. If possible, gutters collecting roof water along a property line eave should not drain onto the adjacent property. Shed roofs with high points along the ZLL will drain easily onto the original property. Roofs pitching front to rear on a lot can be drained onto the original property, but disposal of the runoff from the rear of lots may present a complication in design. The runoff from roofs draining to either side of the dwelling can be accommodated, with or without gutters, through drainage easements that are established by covenants or deed restrictions.

Special thought should be given to roofs in heavy snowfall areas to avoid slopes which could dump great piles of snow onto adjacent property, causing damage to plantings, fences, or exterior decks. Stacks and vents should be hidden from street views as much as possible. Usually vent pipes can be offset horizontally an adequate distance so that they may be hidden from the street view.

6-13 With the higher densites of ZLL, more simple roof lines can create a less cluttered appearance.

Garages

Small lots and compact, enclosed living areas common to ZLL usually afford little storage area. This fact makes an enclosed garage, as opposed to an open carport, almost a necessity if a pleasant streetscape and quality community are to be maintained. A carport may be designed with proper screening from the street, plus enclosed built-in storage, but the contents often overflow beyond the barrier and an unsightly view is created. In "affordable housing" a carport in lieu of a garage can save dollars, which is very important. However, the potential unpleasant streetscape which can be created by carports can cause an unfortunate stigma on "close" housing concepts and can affect resales. The owners of "affordable" or low-income housing cannot afford such losses. If possible, the garage should be designed for at least one but preferably two vehicle spaces plus storage area. The HUD minimum property standards may serve as an absolute minimum guide to determine the area of both garage size and the outdoor storage area. Garages 16 feet x 18 feet and 18 feet x 18 feet should be considered for markets using smaller cars and where basements provide storage.

The garage door is so prominent in the ZLL streetscape that it really requires special design considerations. Until the trees grow and the landscaping begins to soften and hide some of the buildings in a new project, the streetscape can look like a staccato of garage doors. Therefore, the doors must have design interest. A low roof line at the street facade creates a more open feeling than, for instance, a gable roof or two-story garage (the second story being living spaces). Many developers of ZLL and cluster programs prefer the single-story front with steep sloping roofs to second levels. However, design treatment or emphasis on other aspects can be just as acceptable.

Design emphasis should be for an interesting variety of garage facades and roofs for each unit so that a pleasant streetscape can be created. Design the garage doors with some detail in order to break up the monotony of the large flat surface. Variations in panels, trim, and siding will contribute interest. Lighting fixtures well chosen and well placed can create interest on an otherwise plain facade.

6-14 Design emphasis should be for an interesting variety of garage facades and roofs for units so that a pleasant streetscape can be created.

6-15 and 6-16 Garages and driveways may serve a variety of functions, depending on locality, climate, and regional preference. Care should be taken to protect the streetscene from adverse impacts of garage utilization.

Entrances

Entrances may also be very visible in the streetscape whether they be an entrance door or entrance gate in a privacy fence or wall. The designer has an opportunity to create an inviting entrance, as well as add variety and interest to the streetscape (an element that makes standard setbacks less important). The walls can be designed with interest and character. Preference is for interesting structural design rather than color changes, though both can be successful. Noise penetration should be considered. Wall heights of five and six feet predominate though many have been successful with low to no walls, but with interesting landscape.

Entrance doors can recede into the unit or project out from the facade, be around to the side and out of view, be covered with protective roof or cover, be tied to the garage with a trellised or landscaped walk, or be inviting with an endless variety of design ideas. The doors or gates and light fixtures should be chosen as design features with special emphasis on color and shapes. Garden gate entrances are always an inviting feature and should be highly visible. They do not occur very often in the lower price ranges, however. If the main entrance into the unit is through the courtyard, security of some type at the gate can be incorporated into the design.

6-17 Entranceways can be combined with driveways in ZLL, thus allowing more efficient use of the narrower yard and a more pleasant arrangement of ground plane materials, as shown at Cedarwood, Boca Raton, Florida.

6-18 ZLL arrangements can provide opportunities for private, inviting entrances.

From the entrance door, views into the unit are important, especially to gain sales appeal. Views through a room and beyond to a garden or court are epecially appealing and create a very spacious and open design feeling. Views focusing on special features such as fireplaces or stairways are always interesting. Avoid dull views of plain walls which create a crowded feeling. Above all, avoid views into a bathroom or powder room. With all the possibilities of private, interestingly landscaped small courts that can be planned into the units, attractive views from the entrance door should be easily accomplished. When designing entrances, remember to incorporate into the design the location of utility meters, pipes, vents, air conditioners, etc. Research on existing units has shown that these elements have sometimes been forgotten and show up on the entry walls—an unfortunate lapse in design control, which will impact on sales.

The zero wall of an adjacent house can be used for features, sculptures, wall hangings, etc., but is rarely used for such. Since both homeowners have a vested interest in this wall—one structural, the other visual—deed restrictions, covenants, or similar documents should allow such uses.

6-19 and 6-20 Extreme care must be taken with placement of utilities. An otherwise charming entrance may be ruined by pipes, meters, and valves right outside the front door. 6-21 Consideration must also be given to the treatment of the adjacent zero wall. The placement of utilities on this wall can create the same negative impact as placing them in the entranceway.

Interior Spaces

Within any dwelling unit, spaces can be categorized as habitable and nonhabitable spaces. The habitable spaces include the living areas such as living room, dining room, kitchen, bedroom, and family room which require natural light and ventilation. Nonhabitable rooms or spaces include the utility areas such as bathroom, hallway, stairway, laundry room, furnace room, basement, and storage area. These rooms or spaces do not require natural light or natural ventilation. Bathrooms, for instance, may use artificial light and be ventilated by means of an exhaust fan. Such rooms or spaces may be arranged along the lot line wall where no windows are allowed or required by use. All the habitable spaces then may be arranged with light and views into the private spaces of the yard or the open space toward the street.

In order to increase natural lighting and ventilation in the habitable rooms, interior courtyards or atriums completely open to the sky (or skylights) may be inserted. This arrangement adds the interest of the outdoor space to the indoor room. Figure 6-22 illustrates an example of an interior court or light-well which opens the interior—and potentially dull—dining space onto natural light and plantings and adds interest to the stairway, as well as supplying natural light and ventilation to the lower level of this split level house. This wonderful combination of spaces—indoor and outdoor—should be fully utilized, especially in ZLL housing on very small lots, to gain the maximum use and interest in all the spaces.

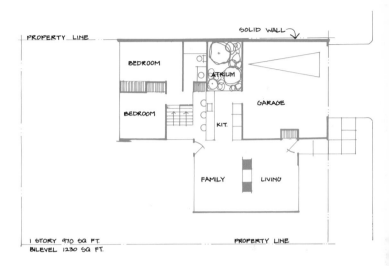

6-22 In order to utilize interior space as habitable rooms, interior courtyards, atriums completely open to the sky, or skylights may be inserted.

Well-placed large areas of glass within rooms can open the interior spaces into much larger exterior spaces—actually borrowing the outdoor space to increase the apparent size of the interior. To make this borrowed space effective, it should be interesting, limited, and private. For instance, the view from a typical urban street window is probably not too interesting, is limited only by walls of buildings across the street or by parked cars, and is certainly not private. Therefore, the inhabitants install draw draperies, curtains, window shades, blinds, or whatever to block out the view and increase privacy. In contrast, the view from a living room in a ZLL house is limited by a large windowless wall. Interest is, therefore, created by landscaping and other outdoor area design. Most importantly, the view is private. Drapes, shades, or blinds are not necessary. In fact, the views into the lighted garden at night are possibly more exciting and desirable than the daytime view with the addition of low level lighting to accent the plants. As discussed in the landscaping section of this book, plantings in these private yards and courts should be designed for year-round interest, especially in the northern climates where deciduous trees and plants lose their foliage in the winter.

This borrowing of space from the outdoors can actually reduce the square footage of

rooms without reducing their desirability or usability. These reductions, in turn, reduce the total square footage of a unit. The smaller unit is of great advantage on the small ZLL lot as it allows for more exterior space for outdoor use. Another obvious advantage is the reduction of total building costs and maintenance because of reduced square footage. This concept should not be overlooked when designing ZLL housing in all price ranges, as this is partially what makes this type of housing attractive.

Typically, living and sleeping areas are separated to create internal privacy for the different functions. The accompanying outdoor areas or courtyards may also be designed to afford the first-floor bedrooms private courts for sunbathing or lounging. Bathrooms opening onto private outdoor areas are very desirable and can be incorporated into the design of luxury units. Windows can be transparent, with views to planted areas—a good sales feature. Hot tubs, whirlpools, and water elements can also be incorporated into these very private outdoor areas.

Second-floor bedrooms and baths create a design problem in the concentrated ZLL concept. It is difficult to place second-floor windows or balconies where they will not allow an open view of neighboring outdoor

6-23 The walls opening onto the private courts in ZLL can be almost totally of glass, greatly expanding the visual size of the rooms. This is especially true for projects in warm climates such as this one in Waipio, Hawaii.

areas. High windows with sills above eye level may offer a solution which allows light and ventilation and limits the view. Long slender windows may help limit the view. Windows onto interior light wells or courtyards offer a good solution, as do windows on the street facade. Units should be sensitively sited to avoid undesirable second-floor views.

Indoor/Outdoor Space Relationships

Another prime consideration to successful planning for ZLL is the relationship of indoor and outdoor spaces requiring close and meticulous coordination between the land planner, landscape architect, and the architect. Very often in traditional single-family development the land planning and actual lotting of a site precedes the architectural involvement of designing specific units. In a ZLL project, if this approach is used, the space relationships may not be well coordinated. Coordination meetings, which should include the land planner, the landscape architect, and the architect should address the following:

Lot-to-lot relationships.

- Drainage patterns
- Elevation variations (contours)
- Vegetation conservation
- Solar orientation potential
- Visual screening potential
- Sound screening potential
- Lot line to building wall locations

Unit floor plan adaptabilities.

- Acceptable footprint for given lot sizes
- Solar orientation potential
- Outdoor area privacy screening

Siting of units.

- Solar orientation
- Indoor/outdoor relationships (privacy, views, noise screening)
- Streetscapes (setbacks, interest interplay between units)
- Construction problems
- Fire fighting access

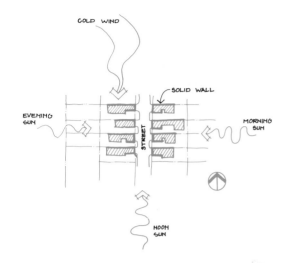

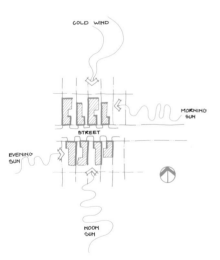

6-24   Unit plans and solar orientation of lots should be coordinated in early design phases. If a majority of the streets run north-south, unit designs can by layed out to best utilize passive or active solar radiation. Notice that the solid zero lot line wall is on the north side of the unit. In some hot climates, it may be better to put the solid wall on the south side of the unit.   6-25   If the streets run east-west then the units will have to be carefully designed to capture the sun.

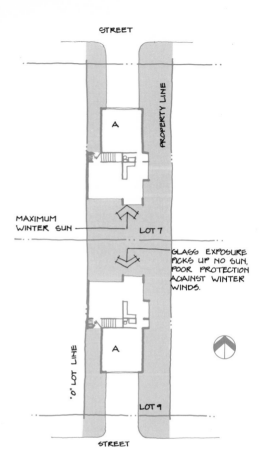

STREET

PROPERTY LINE

A

MAXIMUM
WINTER SUN

LOT 7

GLASS EXPOSURE
PICKS UP NO SUN,
POOR PROTECTION
AGAINST WINTER
WINDS.

'O' LOT LINE

A

LOT 9

STREET

6-26   shows the same unit sited on two back-to-back lots on east-west streets, and the direction of desirable solar orientation for each unit. On Lot 7, Unit A orients perfectly. However, the same Unit A orients poorly on Lot 9. With the variety of units available all of the A units on east-west streets can be sited with the garage oriented north.   6-27   shows the same Unit A sited on lots with north-south streets. The unit sites very well on Lot 16 and the reverse of the unit sites well on Lot 15.

As the housing unit designs progress, the lot-to-lot relationships can be reviewed and reworked to best accommodate the units, and the unit designs can also be tailored to the lotting. For example, lotting and regrading of existing contours may be accomplished to allow for all grading to occur between units, thereby allowing units to be designed on a flat pad. Or, grade changes may be accomplished within the lot which may require split level units to be designed. Unit plans and solar orientation of lots should also be coordinated in the early design phases. If a majority of the streets must of necessity run north-south, unit designs can be layed out to best utilize passive solar or even active solar radiation. Sites on which street alignments are flexible may be planned entirely to create the maximum number of lots with the proper solar orientation. Use of certain predesigned units may either collect or reject the maximum amount of solar radiation. Hopefully in the immediate

future, governmental regulations will permit and encourage all projects to be designed to create lots with maximum orientation to the sun in cold climates and away from the sun in warm climates—a concept which has certainly been overlooked in the past energy-wasting era.

As the unit plans are being developed along with the land planning and lotting, the total team can review and critique the designs to ascertain the adaptability of the footprints to

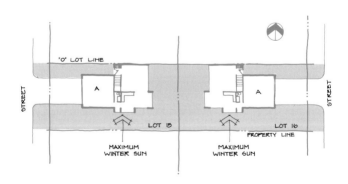

'O' LOT LINE

STREET

A

A

STREET

LOT 15

LOT 16

PROPERTY LINE

MAXIMUM
WINTER SUN

MAXIMUM
WINTER SUN

the lot sizes. Are the footprints too large or too small? Do they site well on the lot? Do the units orient well on the given lots to solar radiation? Can privacy between units be accomplished? If this interplay between the design disciplines can be accomplished during the early design process, a very sensitive, quality project can surface. All too often the land plan is proposed and platted long before any products are designed and the resulting project can show the lack of coordination.

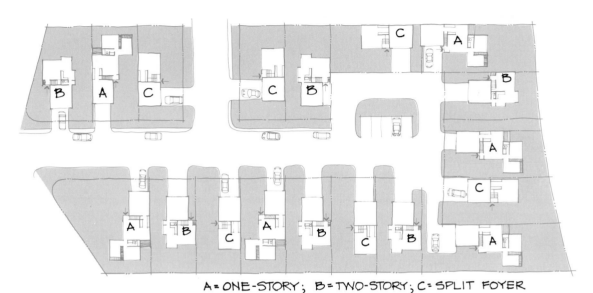

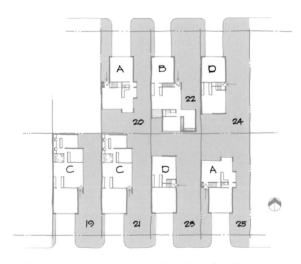

A = ONE-STORY; B = TWO-STORY; C = SPLIT FOYER

6-29   On the 18 lots illustrated, most of the units are set back an adequate distance from the street line to allow cars to be parked in the driveway. This is not a requirement, although with narrow streets and short spaces between driveways, very little street parking may be available or needed. Note that all setbacks are not the same, nor are they repetitious. This avoids the monotony of aligned garage doors, not uncommon in many urban streetscapes. The two-story units break up the vertical monotony of all single-story garage roofs. To add further interest, each unit has an alternate elevation and alternate color scheme. Therefore, the viewer is not really aware of the fact that the street is built with only three different unit floor plans.

6-28   Indoor/outdoor relationships relate directly to views, privacy, and sound transfer. First-floor views are very acceptable if they orient toward solid walls of adjacent units or are blocked by high lot line fences. The private outdoor living areas on Lots 21, 22, and 23 are rather well screened from second-floor Unit A views by the building masses. The building masses also reduce the amount of sound transfer between units and are far more effective as sound barriers than wooden fences between patios of units, such as in 24 and 25. Solid masonry lot line walls create a much better sound baffle as sound does not penetrate masonry. Avoid, whenever possible, adjacent patios separated only by a wood fence, as these patios are the least private soundwise.

6-30   Depending on the size of the side yards and courts, the outdoor spaces can visually expand the interior space and allow light in.

7 Landscape Concepts

Limited space is not detrimental when properly planned and designed. Through the creative use of design elements such as the ground plane, grading, walls, fences, lighting, plants, and solar orientation, the smallest of outdoor areas can function efficiently and quite dramatically as outdoor rooms.

Delineation and separation of outdoor rooms can be achieved with walls, fences, and plant materials; special effects or moods can be created with night lighting, shadow patterns, and color; and climatic comfort can be achieved through the utilization of solar orientation (outdoor use can be extended into the spring and fall), proper plant selection/location, and overhead structures.

7-1 This Woodbridge Gables home demonstrates the advantages of carefully planned landscaping. The landscaping can soften the impact of the higher density structures, delineate space, and provide pleasing surroundings.

Courtyards

The development of courts or small yards for the ZLL project offers a number of desirable advantages. The "forecourt" at the street entry to the ZLL house can add dramatically to the project streetscape in terms of "curb-appeal" for the individual unit and visual interest enrichment. It also creates an aesthetic entrance to the house from the street. A second advantage to the forecourt, in utilizing some hard surfaces, is a cost savings for landscaping with a reduction in blue-grass lawn installation and maintenance. Side yard courts and patios may, as discussed previously, become outdoor extensions of indoor living spaces. Because the small ZLL side yard is functional space, the unit psychologically appears larger.

7-2 and 7-3 Through the creative use of design elements such as ground plane, grading, walls, fences, lighting, plants, and solar orientation, the smallest of outdoor areas can function effectively and quite dramatically as outdoor use areas.

7-4 The development of courts or small yards for the ZLL project offers a number of desirable advantages.

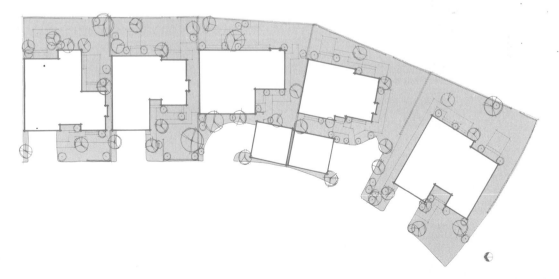

7-5 This masonry wall in Whetstone encloses an entry court adjacent to parking. Impact is lessened through the use of landscaping.

Fences and Walls

Fences can provide residents privacy with increased outdoor use. Fencing defines property boundaries and creates an outdoor "living room" by enclosing the private space. High fencing tightly encloses the space since views are terminated. Low or transparent fencing reduces privacy but allows for a more spacious atmosphere.

7-6 Fences need not be massive, continuous, or of consistent material or design to provide interesting facades and a sense of privacy. There should be some common element between different fences, however, such as color or material, to tie them together visually.

Beyond screening other houses and residents, fencing can mitigate many other undesirable elements such as adjacent highways, roads, shopping centers, dumpsters, on-site trash areas, and on-site mechanical features. Noise from neighbors and traffic can be filtered or blocked with fences and walls and accompanying plant material. Wind created by high density housing can be mitigated or redirected; snow accumulation patterns in cold climates can also be controlled. Off-site residential lighting and automobile headlights can be blocked from view. Finally, fencing helps segregate the private from the public spaces and increases the security control of private facilities.

POOR ADJACENT VIEWS   PUBLIC/PRIVATE PEDESTRIAN SPACE

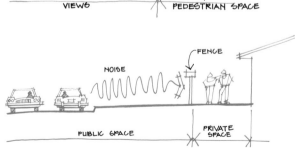

NOISE   FENCE

PUBLIC SPACE   PRIVATE SPACE

7-7 External visual clutter must be blocked from view to allow full enjoyment of private amenities. 7-8 Noise from neighbors and traffic can be filtered or blocked by fences and walls.

As a landscape detail, fencing has a major impact upon the visual environment.

- Fencing adds three dimensional form, color, line, and texture to the landscape.
- Each fence has a different impact. Consider the effect on landscape character of a four-foot-high wrought iron fence garnished with brick pilasters, versus the effect of a six-foot-high rough-cut cedar screen.
- Fencing can effectively divide a horizontal surface into two or more spaces, providing visual privacy within each space.
- Fencing can define separate spaces while retaining visual continuity.
- Fencing can establish an entire theme for a landscape; for example, a split-rail fence sets a rural character while a

white picket fence creates an old-time residential touch.

- Existing architectural concepts can be extended into the landscape or complemented by appropriate fence detailing. For example, a wrought iron fence complements a classic brick house or estate while a contemporary rough-cut cedar siding home may best be extended into the landscape by using a low fence, constructed out of similar material.

Fencing and walls are often prohibitively expensive, though. As a result, they should be used judiciously. If, in order to meet costs, fencing is installed which demands annual maintenance and repairs, it should not be used. On the other hand, deletion of backyard fencing in a high density housing project may make privacy impossible.

7-9 and 7-10 Existing architectural concepts can be extended into the landscape or complimented by appropriate fencing. At Whetstone, the unit walls are extended to enclose courtyards. 7-11 At Country Walk, the horizontal siding of the units is utilized in the fence design.

7-12, 7-13, and 7-14 Privacy fences used in front yards or side yards facing a collector road can provide additional privacy as well as add another dimension of interest to street frontages.

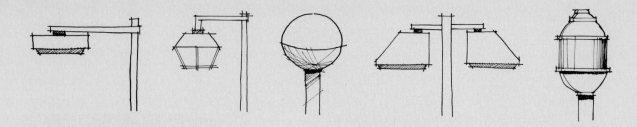

7-15 The selected light standard for a residential community can portray a theme or "image" throughout the development.

Lighting

Site lighting provides a residential community with character, security, extension of outdoor use time, and visual aesthetics. The selected light standard can portray a theme throughout the community. In some areas it is appropriate to utilize the light fixture as a visual element, in contrast to other areas where it is desirable to have a hidden light source. For example, decorative lighting at community/public facilities may provide sparkle or accent to public spaces. Lighting for circulation (vehicular and pedestrian)

may be most effective in illuminating the ground plane while concealing the light source. Lighting is important in ZLL developments since due to the compactness of the lots, the street becomes a more important common open space.

When streets are dedicated to a municipality, standard city fixtures are normally required, though some utility companies offer alternatives. It is advantageous to investigate other available lighting standards/fixtures to establish visual continuity that enhances community image. Often a homeowners' association can take over the responsibility if a better lighting system is desired.

Community privacy in ZLL developments for the residential homeowner can be achieved through the use of specialty fixtures with "cut-off" illumination patterns. These fixtures avoid street glare into residential units and their private outdoor spaces. Areas requiring more intense lighting, such as recreation

7-16 and 7-17 Lighting must be adequate for safety and security, but must be kept in scale with the ZLL project.

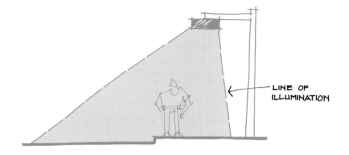

LINE OF ILLUMINATION

7-18 Community privacy is achieved through the use of specialty features with "cut-off" illumination patterns.

clubs, parks, or model complexes, when adjacent to residential areas, should also use cut-off fixtures.

Selection of light standards and fixtures should be based upon a criteria addressing initial construction cost, long-term maintenance, and resistance to vandalism. Very often, the intensity of light is too high as proposed using traditional standards for light levels. A lower intensity may be satisfactory as well as energy conserving.

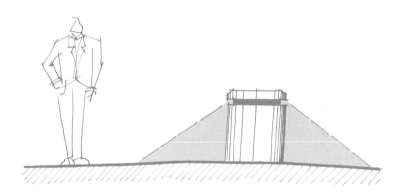

7-19 The quality of lighting at the zero lot line street scale must be safe lighting, avoiding glare from light sources. For pedestrian areas, subdued lighting which focuses upon illuminating the ground plane is more appropriate. Sometimes accent lighting of plant materials is also appropriate.

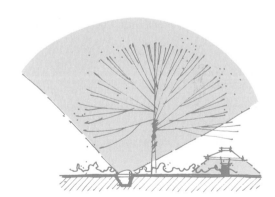

93

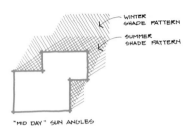

WINTER
SHADE PATTERN

SUMMER
SHADE PATTERN

"MID DAY" SUN ANGLES

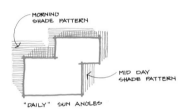

MORNING
SHADE PATTERN

MID DAY
SHADE PATTERN

"DAILY" SUN ANGLES

7-20   In order to gain maximum usage from the small courtyards and deck areas in ZLL projects, these spaces should be oriented toward or away from the sun, depending on the climate.

SUN ANGLE
VARIATION

7-21   Deciduous trees correspond to summer/winter sun angles by blocking out unwanted summer sun, while allowing winter sun to shine through, once leaves have dropped.

Solar Orientation

Solar access is critical to optimum usability of the outdoor spaces within the various climates. For example, east oriented patios are shaded from the hot summer sun, providing a pleasant outdoor use area in late afternoon and evening. In milder climates, an outdoor use area of southern exposure may be used year-round. In colder climates the southern exposure may extend use of outdoor spaces into the fall and spring.

7-22   The overhead trellis at this Sea Pines house offers shade and adds an additional dimension to the outside of the structure.   7-23   Overhead structures and plant materials can modify temperatures and create a micro-climate in the courtyard. The trellis in this Woodbridge Gables courtyard also provided interesting textures in the shadow on the court floor.

Other ways to modify temperature involve the use of overhead structures and plant materials. These design items can create an effective overhead plane that modifies the effect of the sun in varying degrees. Designing the height of permanent overhead structures, such as trellises, to correspond to winter/summer sun angles can block out unwanted summer sun but let in winter warmth. Deciduous trees serve the same function by dropping their leaves and allowing the winter sun to shine through. Adjacent dwelling units must also be analyzed in determining reflected light, heat gain, and shade opportunities.

Light colored surfaces reflect heat and light and are cooler than dark surfaces, but glare is a problem. Darker surfaces absorb heat, are hot in the summer, warm in the winter sun, and glare is less of a problem. Patterns of sun and shade across an outdoor living space create an interesting surface and offer a choice of temperature for sitting or playing.

Use of small water elements can modify the micro-climate of patio areas. The sound of water splashing has a cooling effect. Water areas can trap heat during the day for release in the evening. However, water surfaces can cause glare problems.

Resource Conscious Design

Application of sound landscape architecture and landscape design principles can result in a resource conscious design, producing energy savings and subsequent savings in maintenance dollars. Resource conscious design principles include judicious use of water, gasoline, and personnel time for maintenance and fertilizer application. Additionally, design principles such as providing shade for a wall with trees and shrubs can reduce heating and cooling costs for the residential homeowner. Plants also can enhance views from within the house as well as block unwanted views. Specifically, conserving resources through planting design employs utilization of plant groupings by water requirements and maintenance requirements (i.e., group plants having similar water needs so that a planting may not be overwa-

tered to meet the needs of a higher water requirement plant material).

In the ZLL project, extension of outdoor courts and decks can effectively reduce one of the most resource-wasteful elements of the traditional landscape—the sod lawn. Lawns use large amounts of water and fertilizer and require substantial maintenance. The use of other groundcovers and paving can be considered as an alternative to sod. In areas of short water supply, drought resistant plant materials, such as natives or hearty introduced plants, can be used.

To reduce maintenance time and costs, carefully locate or avoid plantings that drop fruits or flowers. Also, use primarily long-lived hearty plants rather than quick-growing, short-lived, or exotic plants that need frequent replacement.

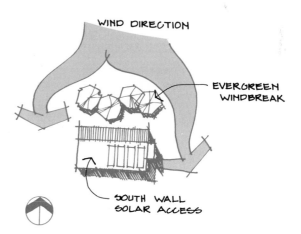

7-24 Tree masses divert and weaken winter winds that would steal warmth from houses.

The Ground Plane

The ground plane (i.e., driveway, courts, lawns, walks) is one of the most important dimensions used to define space. This surface, hard or soft, living or not, offers opportunity for texture, pattern, color, and form as well as necessary utilitarian aspects such as providing access and direction to the surrounding environment.

The ground plane becomes increasingly important in zero lot line development because as setbacks are smaller, detail becomes more obvious. From the street, visual continuity is imperative. The number of curb cuts needs to be kept to a minimum. Garage facades, driveways, and entrance walkways should be simple, attractive, and harmonious in appearance. Planted areas need to relate one to another in continuous order versus clutter.

7-25, 7-26, and 7-27 Paving patterns can visually enlarge an area while creating a sense of scale. 7-28 A small pattern often yields the greatest scale and detail, as in Patio C. Patio A could be any size and scale.

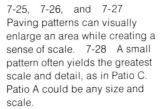

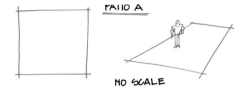

PATIO A

NO SCALE

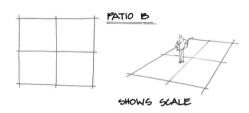

PATIO B

SHOWS SCALE

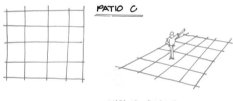

PATIO C

SHOWS SCALE
AND DETAIL

The overall project image can be enhanced by retaining as much greenery as possible to be viewed from the street. Common areas need to convey visual continuity by repetition of basic ground plane patterns, such as grass panels or other ground covers. This approach in ZLL projects carried forth in all common areas can make open space flow throughout the project, linking various parts together, in essence "stitching" the parts together to form a cohesive whole.

Public walks also should reinforce the concept of creating a common ground plane through consistent use of similar materials (form, color, texture). Emphasis should be placed upon low maintenance, such as concrete versus bomanite, flagstone, or brick in sand. Material installation should be of common construction practice to allow lower initial improvement costs. Sidewalks should be kept to absolute minimums (three feet), should occur on only one side of the street, or be eliminated on loops and cul-de-sacs where traffic is minimized. They should accommodate pedestrians only.

Sophisticated paving materials should occur at project focal areas such as the recreation center/clubhouse and unit entrances. These areas have the potential for setting examples for the ZLL project in terms of appropriate use of materials (i.e., parking, planting, irrigation, signage, and decorative lighting).

In the ZLL project, private spaces provide an opportunity for detailed project enrichment and individuality. Specifically, at the private level, those outdoor spaces become increasingly significant in conveying scale or spatial delineation. Paving, for example, can visually enlarge a space by use of a smaller modular grid; the small module (i.e., bricks, concrete pavers, 2 x 4 decking versus 2 x 6) can make a space appear larger as well as add a level of intimacy. Small spaces can therefore take on pleasant feelings by added detail in paving or decking. Decking can also be broken up into smaller grid patterns to create intimacy and spaciousness.

Thus, paving can play a major role in delineating public versus private space by its level of detail and jointery. Public paving (walks) by contrast should be simple materials (concrete) with larger modular grids (trowel joints). The design of common area spaces and the private spaces in the model complex are the developer's means of conveying to the buyer appropriate scale and materials.

Streetscape

The streetscape development is extremely critical for the ZLL development, particularly so since the smaller lot configuration associated with this kind of development draws attention to the linear street right-of-way. The opportunity exists to make this parkway (i.e., asphalt edge to right-of-way line) area an identifiable area—a contributing element to the neighborhood and an element which creates visual continuity as a linking agent.

The front yard setback in ZLL concepts is normally smaller than standard subdivision (five to 18 feet) though it can be the same. This is not a negative. Instead, it is used as a selling feature (less maintenance) and can be developed more intensely than standard projects given the same budget. Also, less goes farther. The linear parkway in front of the individual ZLL homes should be designed to convey "sense of place" to the viewer: regular spacing of street trees, attached sidewalk (if needed and functional) at minimum dimensions, and placement of street signage for ease of readability. "Sense of place" and visual identity may further be delineated by focusing on simple efficient design of common elements such as light standards, mail boxes, and location and dimensions of driveways to minimize their attendant curb cuts. Special landscape features, particularly at the entrance to neighborhoods or the project itself and in enclaves within the project, can lend identity.

7-29   Streetscape design can be very important to the success of ZLL. This curvilinear street in Boca West presents a pleasing view.

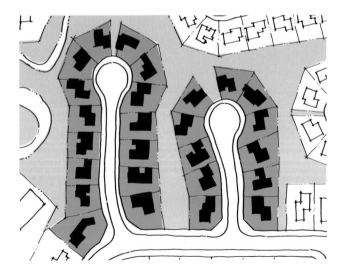

7-30   Placement of units on the lots can be extremely varied in order to create a good streetscape composition.

7-31   Even potentially pleasant streetscape designs can be spoiled in actual use. Inadequate driveways for off-street parking can cause this sort of cluttered streetscene. Narrower pavement and curved streets can improve the visual quality.

7-32   Varied and interesting facades can produce a pleasant streetscene. This development utilizes side entry garages in order to avoid direct views into the garage. Note the absence of sidewalks and the use of minimal curbs and gutters.

7-33, 7-34 and 7-35 An important aspect to the overall streetscene is the size, design, and placement of mailboxes. A much more pleasing scene can be created by the use of coordinated mailboxes, with several combined on one post. 7-34 and 7-35 show poor solutions to mailbox placement and design.

Driveways can become the single most visual element to the streetscape. The closeness of curb cuts and driveways can interrupt the visual continuity of the landscaped parkway. They can become too dominant. Similarly, parked cars in driveways may have a like effect if driveway design does not permit enough room for the auto length in front of garages; the resultant blockage can create "visual clutter" by blocking sidewalks and parkways. Many projects are designed to eliminate parking from in front of the garages. In some, door openings predominate. The design and location of driveways is therefore a critical factor for ZLL development streetscape. Where costs allow, driveways can be broken up with turf area or patterned for greater interest through the use of heavy landscaping, street trees, decorative fencing, distinctive mail boxes, entrance features, and minimal concrete or similar material.

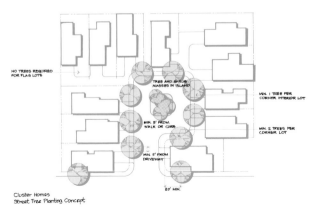

Cluster Homes
Street Tree Planting Concept

7-36   Street tree planting concept for zero lot line homes.

7-37   The streetscape development is extremely critical for ZLL development. The linear parkway in front of the individual homes should be designed to carry a "sense of place."

7-38 and 7-39   Attractive signage also contributes to a pleasing streetscape.

7-40 and 7-41 Use of retaining walls can create additional level space within the ZLL yard. When made of appropriate materials and incorporated as part of the landscape, they can also provide increased value.

Retaining Walls

There are many practical benefits retaining walls provide beyond the primary soil retention function. However, it should be noted that due to their costs, sites for ZLL should be selected that avoid or minimize their use.

Many sloped areas that are difficult to maintain can achieve easier development and maintenance by the installation of retaining walls. These are then more manageable because access to planting beds and sodded areas is made easier through the construction of walls. The initial costs of retaining walls are high, but conditions that are cor-rected by the construction of walls are often more cost effective to maintain. Retaining walls usually become long-term solutions to a grade problem, and if constructed proper-ly, will last for years. The construction methods used in retaining walls are critical to allow for the natural water flow and drain-age of the retained area to pass through the wall. The process of slope reduction not only minimizes soil erosion, but also significantly reduces water runoff and eventual consump-tion of water in the irrigated areas. It also can reduce the cost of on- and off-site drain-age facilities.

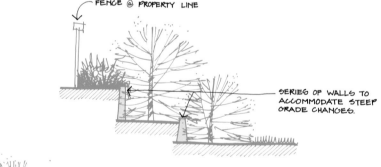

FENCE @ PROPERTY LINE

SERIES OF WALLS TO ACCOMMODATE STEEP GRADE CHANGES.

7-42 Planting beds are made more manageable due to a series of retaining walls. 7-43 The use of retaining walls permits segregation of adjacent land uses, while eliminating the need for fencing. 7-44 Special use areas, such as model home complexes, recreation clubs, and pocket parks, may have their functional spaces/ activities physically and visually separated with retaining walls.

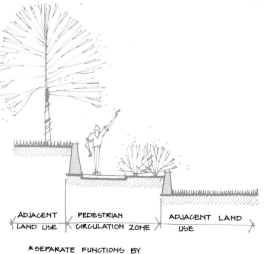

ADJACENT LAND USE | PEDESTRIAN CIRCULATION ZONE | ADJACENT LAND USE

*SEPARATE FUNCTIONS BY VERTICAL GRADE CHANGES.

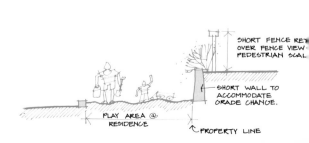

SHORT FENCE RET OVER FENCE VIEW PEDESTRIAN SCAL

SHORT WALL TO ACCOMMODATE GRADE CHANGE.

PLAY AREA @ RESIDENCE

PROPERTY LINE

The use of retaining walls in steep slope situations can permit ZLL development which would otherwise be unfeasible. Functional driveways, patios, and elements of the dwelling unit can be maintained on a relatively horizontal plane with closer placement. Use of retaining walls can generate more usable level space within the small lot configuration. The higher installation cost of retaining walls must be weighed against project economics.

Retaining walls may, depending on their height, clearly define exterior spaces. They may easily be used to control access between levels. Retaining walls in combination with fencing provide privacy. Their use may provide one opportunity to segregate automobile and pedestrian circulation. Such walls may eliminate the need for the fencing of small spaces common to ZLL concepts; this may also enhance a space by making it appear larger without the traditional fencing enclosure. Where a retaining wall is needed, its proper design as more than a wall can create a premium value for the ZLL lot.

Special use areas, such as model home complexes, recreation clubs, and pocket parks, may have their functional spaces/activities physically and visually delineated by grade separations with attendant retaining walls. For example, in parks, seating areas may be built into walls separating active areas from a passive area. A retaining wall may physically separate an active area such as a swimming pool from a terraced seating area for quiet contemplation. Additionally, in this case, the wall may provide a degree of privacy screening the adjacent residential land use.

The commonly used materials for retaining walls are:

- Large rocks or boulders
- Wrapped rocks in bundles
- Wood timbers
- Railroad ties
- Brick
- Concrete block
- Concrete poured-in-place or precast.

The type of retaining wall can either complement the architecture or become an extension of it. This relationship to the architecture is especially important in ZLL situations because the units are close together.

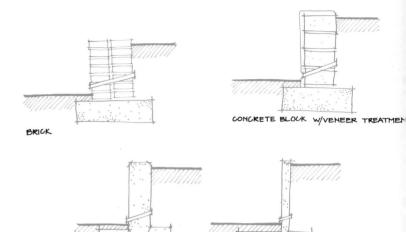

BRICK

CONCRETE BLOCK W/VENEER TREATMEN

POURED-IN-PLACE CONCRETE

PRECAST CONCRETE PANELS

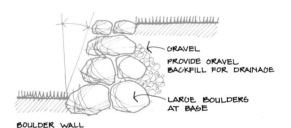

GRAVEL

PROVIDE GRAVEL BACKFILL FOR DRAINAGE

LARGE BOULDERS AT BASE

BOULDER WALL

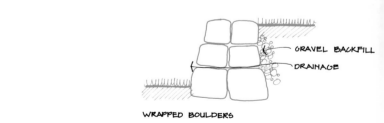

GRAVEL BACKFILL

DRAINAGE

WRAPPED BOULDERS

7-45 Boulders, brick, and concrete are commonly used materials for retaining walls. Retaining walls can complement or extend the architecture of units.

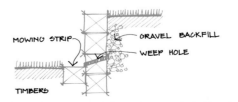

MOWING STRIP

GRAVEL BACKFILL

WEEP HOLE

TIMBERS

101

8 Construction Considerations

Certain construction problems may be encountered by the builder of ZLL units which may not be common to single-family or townhouse construction. Since alleys or greenspace are not required between the rear walls of units, there may be no space available to move excavation machinery, concrete trucks, or backfill equipment behind the units. Side yards may be minimal and cause the same problems. Workable areas in the street may also be diminished because of the zero or minimum setbacks from the front lot lines which may create very real delivery and storage problems. When programming the construction process, the entire construction site should be studied with the total construction team in order to properly plan and program the following:

- utility installations
- excavation
- concrete delivery
- backfilling
- material storage
- framing
- landscaping
- street and walk construction.

8-1 Certain construction problems may be encountered by the builder of ZLL units which may not be common to other single-family or townhouse construction. The closeness of the units makes it difficult for machinery to pass through. Also, while basements may be desirable in certain markets, they may create difficult construction problems for ZLL developments.

Available spaces between adjacent units, whether back-to-back and/or side-to-side, will probably dictate the direction the construction process. The process may be started at the rear of the lots and progress toward the street, or start at one end of a group of lots and work parallel to the streets. In any event, plan ahead.

It is important to plan also for the equipment necessary to construct rear and side yard fences or walls and landscaping within the lots. If large trees are required at the rear of very small closely constructed lots, it may be necessary to plant them even before excavation is begun to allow for the large equipment access. This may be a very extreme example, but it should serve to strengthen the point being made of preplanning the construction process totally.

While basements may be very desirable in certain markets, they may create undesirable or even impossible construction problems. Certainly the advantage of offering basements as an expansion of living space plus additional storage space is a great sales feature in geographical areas where basements are possible and generally accepted. However, soil conditions and tight construction areas may make it difficult to offer basements. Sandy soils require excessive over-

dig. More expensive construction methods on small lots where distances between basement walls are small may be incurred. Even clay soils which require little overdig are made more difficult if spaces between units are too constricted. It may be difficult for adequately sized machinery to work in the excavated areas; also, space necessary for storage of backfill material and topsoil may be inadequate and difficult to work within. Crawl spaces and lower level areas of split level units may not create the same construction complexities as full basements, since the excavations are not as deep and the amount of space required for backfill material storage is less. Nonetheless, these spaces should also be analyzed with respect to soil conditions and availability of working space. Adequate spacing of rows or groups of units improves access for construction. Alternating rows or groups in construction can also help. Smaller equipment can be utilized when necessary.

Actual construction may include any method of construction, from on-site "stick built" to prefabricated panelized building sections and completely prefabricated units. Local tradition and builder preference usually determine construction types for any given area. "Stick built" or on-site framing may be

most readily adapted to the various lot sizes as well as unit type variations, especially large units on small lots. The materials can be delivered incrementally, piece by piece, and are easily distributed to the required areas through constricted passages or even through the units themselves. Prefabricated panelized building sections, on the other hand, are delivered in large sections and may require cranes for erection. On very small, tightly constructed lots, the delivery and erection may create certain problems which require special planning and programming, such as the crane placement and boom size. Certainly this method of construction has many advantages in the cold climates where construction is planned continuously through the winter season. The actual building of the panels is accomplished in the heated shop and erection can easily be continued throughout the very cold weather. Utilizing totally prefabricated units will take careful preplanning with the manufacturer to coordinate staging and delivery. Space must be available for the delivery trailers adjacent to the foundations to allow the units to be transferred from the trailer onto the foundation. The manufacturer must therefore plan his delivery and frame the units properly so the transfer onto the foundation can be accomplished without causing damage to the unit.

9 Processing

Processing of a ZLL project should not be substantially different from any other project. Project organization involving an experienced consulting team and plan preparation through programming, planning, and design should be identical to other projects. The consulting team should be composed of a land planner, landscape architect, architect, economist, civil engineer, and an attorney. Additional thoroughness, however, should be encouraged in order to sufficiently inform those who must approve the project and those who must accept the project if it is a new concept.

9-1 Through use of interesting building design, well-planned landscaping and ground plane, and attention to details, ZLL can provide residential development superior to standard subdivisions.

Generally, city and county planning departments are capable of dealing with a ZLL project both in terms of developer objectives and intent as well as having the legal tools to handle the task. Agencies which have experienced the ZLL concept numerous times have no difficulty with applying and modifying standard development regulations to the concept. These items may include easements, architectural building envelope sizes, jurisdiction of commons, or project specific street standards. Other agencies may feel more comfortable in using a full PUD procedure which calls for detailed design of all project components. In either case, however, close communication with the public officials is needed because this understanding of small details in a ZLL may have significant cost implications if something has to be "fixed" during the construction stage.

If proposed ZLL development concepts are unique to an area or if people in positions of authority are unfamiliar with the land use type, extra care should be taken to "sell" the project to those who may not be familiar with the ZLL concept. In this instance "selling" will involve a significant educational process. Certainly this publication can be a part of that process. Planners, engineers, members of the planning commission and council, area residents, special interest groups, etc., all need to be educated about the ZLL concept. It may prove desirable to implement an educational program utilizing simplistic graphics which describe the basic concept, architectural models and floor plans, the land plan showing neighborhood improvements and assets, and perhaps project cost analysis. This education process should begin long before the zoning submittal. Public sector acceptance of the concept and, where it is new, willingness to make the accommodation of regulations required, should be achieved before a site commitment is made.

9-2 Maintenance easements between the dwellings can be provided for in the homeowners' covenants or in deed restrictions.

Typical Problems Encountered During Processing	Potential Solutions
Large lot syndrome	• determine cost of development construction per d.u. • determine cost of city services per d.u. • explain lifestyle orientation • explain that ZLL can occur in all lot sizes
Surrounding land use conflicts	• show compatibility with conventional single-family via cost and buyer comparisons • show compatibility with multifamily via density and amenity comparisons • program architectural compatibility • add land use/lot buffer
ZLL concept	• show plan and elevation graphics • show renderings (perspectives)
Smaller is cheaper/less quality	• explain marketing and lifestyle information • discuss architectural components • provide available economic comparisons of existing projects
Recreation requirements	• indicate proximity to existing facilities • discuss on-site facilities
Streetscape clutter	• explain landscape concepts • discuss architectural variations • illustrate proper parking solutions • provide short runs of straight streets
No appropriate zone for project	• adopt project to existing zone • use project as a model to prepare new zone classification
On-the-line problems for the city	• compare with standard housing • allow building code standards for separations
Drainage and maintenance	• provide deed restrictions, convenants, or easements
Why should we make special provisions for this project?	• point out lower costs to buyer • explain energy-saving features • note that traditional requirements are excessive and ZLL is needed

Certainly there is no single formula for success. As with other new ideas from the past, such as clusters, PUDs, and condominiums, the ZLL concept needs to be sold in many areas. The best way to do that is through communication and sound planning. Remember all departments and planning commissions are advisory to the municipal council or county commission. Proceed with this in mind. If the path to approval is not clear, ask that the staff take the ZLL concept to the council or commission for guidance and at the very least try to obtain "approval in principal" before proceeding.

Few communities have standard ZLL zoning classifications and will want to use the PUD or similar classification. A successful project can be developed through PUD; however, it should not be needed, particularly since its use results in added time at extra cost to the consumer. Most communities can accommodate ZLL by adding a provision in all existing or preferred zones to provide for setbacks on side, rear, or front yards with provisions for building separations. The ZLL will look identical to the standard subdivision (except for visual improvements noted in earlier chapters), and each resident will have a more usable lot.

For small lot programs (35 to 50 feet wide) new zones should be adopted with the above provisions for setbacks. The intention is not that this housing does or does not match a preconceived option; it is that it is a needed new option, a good solution, and cost effective housing.

10 Legal Implications

ZLL housing is common in California, Florida, Hawaii, and a few other states, but is limited to special instances in the balance of the nation. (Many older clusters in PUD projects have on-the-line products without many people knowing it.) As a result, most local zoning and subdivision ordinances are not written to permit such development as a standard item, which it should be. In most communities, ZLL housing can be built under planned unit development and/or planned building group ordinances. These more costly processing procedures (in terms of time and money) frequently act as a deterrent to the creation of such projects by builders and developers. Under some ordinances, variances may be used to achieve ZLL projects. In other areas, ZLL projects have been built through use easements and "swapped" easements on standard single-family lots. Through this approach, zoning complications can be avoided; neither a PUD nor variance is necessary. Generally, any project which adopts an open space concept and a homeowners' association will be processed through a PUD. But ZLL development can be built and zoned under standard classifications by altering minimum lot size, setbacks and yard requirements, parking ratios and requirements, bulk plane, site coverage, and open space limits.

10-1 Easements and use of the space between the dwellings need to be spelled out in detail.

Legal questions arising from ZLL development are primarily as a result of the access and maintenance easements needed to maintain the zero walls. Periodic upkeep is essential and can cause disputes between homeowners over the amount of access needed, the damage to the easement, the time of access, and the use of materials and equipment during the maintenance activity. Careful site planning should provide suitable space for equipment and personnel to accomplish maintenance tasks; for instance, easements should be sufficient in size to permit ladders, compressors, and other maintenance equipment to move freely. The description of the right for access over the easement should be clearly written to identify rights of each party and obligations to each party.

In situations where no agreement can be reached by the involved parties (this is rare), methods for arbitration should be defined in the project covenants. Numerous approaches are possible. One example is using a homeowners' association. Each owner can appoint a representative (attorney) to jointly choose a third party who will render an impartial decision. At the outset, both owners need to realize that they have a vested interest in the zero wall, one visual, the other structural. Clear documents and a good orientation before and at the closing avoid misunderstandings.

Each owner's rights pertaining to landscaping, erecting structures, and repairing such items due to possible damage by the other owner should be established. Rights for use of the party wall should be defined: can vines be allowed to grow, can trellises or

10-2 Side yards can be used for a variety of purposes but to avoid disagreements, certain restrictions must be spelled out. Salespeople must have a clear understanding of the ZLL concept and prospective buyers must be provided with detailed regulations.

shelves be attached, what is the responsibility for resulting damage, and can the builder attach a trellis or sculpture during construction?

The need for a homeowners' association (HOA) will vary, depending upon the development concept. If common areas are included, then an HOA will usually be required. If common maintenance of grounds and/or buildings is a goal (maintenance of the building and front yards is common in the Chicago area), then, again, the HOA will be needed. However if the ZLL units are planned as a standard subdivision, the HOA can be eliminated. (ULI publications concerning community associations should be referred to for more detail on formation, management, and effectiveness.) It is sufficient to note that HOAs can be or may not be a part of a ZLL development, but the decision

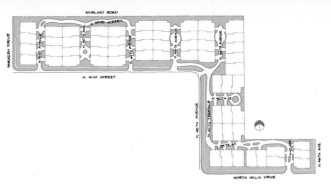

10-3 Subdivision regulations typically are not well suited to or intended for ZLL projects. Excessive street standards, lot line configurations, and easement requirements are possible impediments to a quality ZLL project.

should be made early in the design program. Some HOAs maintain the front yard and exterior of the building (painting each five years, etc.) as well as open space. If an HOA is eliminated, special attention should be paid to unit maintenance procedures, and any park or open space must be dedicated and maintained (for better or worse) by a governmental entity.

Property covenants can be vital to project success. The maintenance of property values is the primary objective of covenants and they should be written with that regard. Covenants can be enforced either through their adoption in a PUD zone ordinance (giving enforcement to the governmental agency), inclusion in an HOA (giving enforcement to the HOA board), or inclusion as deed restrictions that run with each lot (that have virtually no enforcement procedures). The first approach is the most permanent, reliable, and least costly to homeowners. However, the timeliness of city enforcement can be a detriment.

Legal implications of ZLL housing are unique with regard to the zero wall, but the balance of the implications are typical of all other subdivisions, with and without HOAs. Sales agents (and resale agents) must thoroughly understand the ZLL concept and covenants so that full disclosure of property rights and limitations are made prior to sale. 109

Appendices

Appendix A

Declaration of Covenants, Conditions, and Restrictions
Turtle Rock Ridge, Orange County, California
Article XIII
Easements

Section 4 - Certain Easements for Owners

(c) Side-Yard Easements. There is hereby reserved to Declarant, together with the right to grant and transfer the same to the Owners of the Lots described as "Dominant Tenement" on Exhibit G, side-yard easements as shown on said Exhibit, which easements shall be appurtenant to the Lots described on said Exhibit as "Dominant Tenement," and which easements shall burden the Lots described on Exhibit G as "Servient Tenement." Such side-yard easement shall extend over the portion of the Servient Tenement lying between the boundary of the Dominant Tenement and any wall or fence constructed on the Servient Tenement for the purposes of landscaping, drainage, the establishment of a general recreational or garden area and purposes related thereto subject to the following provisions, provided that any such wall or fence on the Servient Tenement shall be deemed to run from the rear boundary of such Lot to the front property line thereof, whether or not such wall or fence actually runs the entire length of such Lot:

(i) The Owner of the Servient Tenement shall have the right at all reasonable times to enter upon the easement area, including the right to cross over the Dominant Tenement for such entry, in order to perform work related to the use and maintenance of the Servient Tenement;

(ii) The Servient Tenement shall have the right of drainage over, across and upon the easement area for water draining from the roof of any dwelling or structure upon the Servient Tenement, the right to maintain eaves and appurtenances thereto and the portions of any dwelling structure upon the Servient Tenement as originally constructed or as constructed pursuant to the Article hereof entitled "Architectural Control";

(iii) The Owner of the Dominant Tenement shall not attach any object to a wall or dwelling belonging to the Servient Tenement or disturb the grading of the easement area or otherwise act with respect to the easement area in any manner which would damage the Servient Tenement;

(iv) In exercising the right of entry upon the easement area as provided for above, the Owner of the Servient Tenement agrees to utilize reasonable care not to damage any landscaping or other items existing in the easement area; provided, however, the Owner of the Servient Tenement shall not be responsible for damage to such landscaping or other items to the extent such damage could not be reasonably avoided in connection with such entry upon the easement area for authorized purposes; and

(v) Except for roof drainage as hereinabove provided, the Owner of the Servient Tenement shall not have the right to concentrate drainage from the Servient Tenement in, under, through or across the easement area without the prior written approval of the Owner of the Dominant Tenement which written approval must be recorded in the Official Records of Orange County, California. Thereafter the Owner of the Ser-

vient Tenement shall have the right of entry upon the easement area for the installation and the subsequent maintenance and repair of such drainage system, providing that any damage to the landscaping or other items existing in the easement area will be repaired at the sole expense of the Owner of the Servient Tenement as soon as reasonably possible following the completion of such installation, maintenance or repair.

(vi) In the event of any dispute arising concerning the rights and obligations created by this Section, the Owner of the Servient Tenement and the Owner of the Dominant Tenement shall each choose one (1) arbitrator, and such arbitrator shall choose one (1) additional arbitrator, and the decision of a majority of all the arbitrators shall be binding upon such Owners.

Protective Covenants And Restrictions
Kingston Dunes Phase II
Shipyard Plantation
Hilton Head, South Carolina
(Partial)
Patio Walls*

2. Dwelling units constructed on said lots must be constructed so as to utilize a Patio Wall. Said Patio Wall shall be constructed simultaneously with the Patio Home and shall be located so that the exterior of the same shall be located three (3) feet inside of and parallel to the lot line as may be designated on the recorded subdivision plat, except that where such

designation is not shown, then the Patio Wall shall be located three (3) feet inside of and parallel to such lot line as may be approved by the Company, its designated agent, successors or assign[or]s through the plans approval process. The dwelling unit shall utilize a portion of the Patio Wall as one of its exterior walls (unless an alternative location of the dwelling is approved pursuant to the other provisions of these covenants) and shall be constructed so that neither the Patio Wall nor the dwelling unit provides any window or view openings looking into or overviewing the adjacent lot and provides no access way or entry way into said adjacent lot. The cost of construction, maintenance and repair of the Patio Wall shall be the sole responsibility of the lot owner on whose lot the same is situated.

3. Should an owner of a Patio Lot desire to locate his Patio Home on a portion of the lot other than contiguous to the Patio Wall, he may apply to the Company, its designated agent, successors or assign[or]s for approval of the alternative location. A site plan showing the proposed alternative location shall accompany such application. The company's approval, or the approval of its designed agent, successors or assign[or]s, of the alternative location shall not relieve the owner's responsibility to construct a Patio Wall as required by Paragraph Two (2). Approval or disapproval of an application for alternative location of a Patio Home may be based by the Company, its designated agent, successors or assign[or]s on purely aesthetic considerations.

*Blank Walls

Easements

5. There is hereby reserved a three (3) foot easement on each lot between the exterior of the Patio Wall and/or residence and the parallel lot boundary line for the use and enjoyment of the adjacent lot owner, only as hereinafter provided. Said three (3) foot easement area and the exterior of the Patio Wall and/or residence may be used by an adjacent lot owner for construction of privacy walls, planting and care of shrubbery and other landscaping, providing the same does not interfere with the structural integrity of the Patio Wall and/or dwelling unit. Said easement shall not apply on those lots in which a Party Wall serves as a portion of the Patio Wall.

6. A five (5) foot easement is further reserved along the boundary line of each lot opposite the boundary line along which the Patio Wall is to be constructed, for the construction, maintenance and repair of the Patio Wall and/or dwelling unit on the adjoining lot. The use of said easement area by an adjoining lot owner shall not exceed a reasonable period of thirty (30) days each year for essential maintenance. Any shrubbery or planting in the five (5) foot easement area that is removed or damaged by the adjoining lot owner during the construction, maintenance or repair of his Patio Wall and/or dwelling unit, shall be repaired or replaced at the expense of the said adjoining lot owner causing such damages. Said easement shall not apply to those lots on which a Party Wall has been constructed.

7. The Company reserves unto itself, its designated agent, successors and assign[or]s alienable and releaseable easements and rights on, over and under the ground to erect, maintain and use utility service and equipment in and over the ten (10) feet of land adjacent to each side of each property line of such area as will be shown by reference to the plats of Shipyard Plantation, save and except that only a three (3) foot easement is reserved adjacent to the property line adjacent to the Patio Wall.

Gentry-Waipio
Deed Form for Lelipua II

Exhibit A

Item I. Description of Sideyard Easement serving Lot No. _____

The Sideyard Easement serving Lot _____ (hereinafter referred to as the "Dominant Estate") shall include all of the area of that certain Easement No. _____ over and across Lot _____ (hereinafter referred to as the "Servient Estate") as shown on Map 533, filed with Land Court Application 1000.

The Sideyard Easement shall be for the exclusive use and enjoyment of the owner of the Dominant Estate and neither the whole nor any part thereof nor any right to use and enjoy the whole or any part thereof shall be sold, mortgaged, leased, rented or otherwise granted and conveyed separate and apart from the Dominant Estate. The Sideyard Easement shall be for the purposes of planting, landscaping, installation and use of general landscape type structures, including such structures as benches, ponds, walks, fences or trellises, general recreation, access, drainage and other visual, aesthetic and recreational purposes and shall be maintained by the owner of the Dominant Estate, as if the area of the Sideyard Easement were owned by the owner of the Dominant Estate, PROVIDED that the owner of the Dominant Estate shall not:

1. suffer or permit any waste upon the Sideyard Easement;

2. undertake any use of or affix any object to any wall, fence or other structure on the Servient Estate which abuts or adjoins the Sideyard Easement;

3. maintain any landscaping or undertake any grading that would tend to prevent proper drainage of the Sideyard Easement, or to promote soil erosion or to undermine support for the foundation of any wall, fence or other structure on the Servient Estate which abuts or adjoins the Sideyard Easement;

4. place or permit the accumulation of any soil or fill material against any wall, fence or other structure on the Servient Estate which abuts or adjoins the Sideyard Easement to a height which exceeds original building permit specifications with regard to grade;

5. permit trees, shrubbery or other vegetation to grow on the Sideyard Easement which would cause damage to or interfere with the maintenance and repair of any wall, fence or other structure on the Servient Estate which abuts or adjoins the Sideyard Easement;

6. cause, suffer or permit any damage to any utility lines located within the Sideyard Easement or interrupt or interfere with the maintenance and repair thereof;

7. cause or permit any offensive contact (including without limitation thereto, any pounding or bouncing of objects) with any wall, fence or other structure on the Servient Estate which abuts or adjoins the Sideyard Easement;

8. suffer or permit upon the Sideyard Easement any activity by household pets or other animals which would tend to cause damage to or undermine support for any wall, fence or other structure on the Servient Estate which abuts or adjoins the Sideyard Easement;

9. cause or permit to exist any open, uncontained fire on the Sideyard Easement;

10. deposit, store or keep any trash, waste or rubbish or containers or receptacles therefore, on any portion of the Sideyard Easement; or

11. construct, erect or install any structure upon, across, over, under or within the Sideyard Easement or undertake any grading or fill or any other activity upon the Sideyard Easement which is in violation or which would result in a violation of any applicable governmental statute, ordinance, rule or regulation;

and PROVIDED, FURTHER, that there shall be reserved to the owner of the Servient Estate with respect to the Sideyard Easement Area the right to:

1. enter upon the Sideyard Easement Area at reasonable times and under reasonable circumstances for the purpose of constructing, reconstructing, maintaining and repairing any fence, wall or other structure on the Servient Estate which abuts or adjoins the Sideyard Easement;

2. permit reasonable drainage of water from the Servient Estate over, upon and across the Sideyard Easement; and

3. cause or permit the foundations of the dwelling constructed upon the Servient Estate to extend under the Sideyard Easement and to cause or permit the eaves and gutters, if any, of the dwelling constructed upon the Servient Estate to extend over the Sideyard Easement at heights no less and extension distances no greater than as such as eaves and gutters are originally constructed; provided that no such gutters shall be permitted which cause or lead to excess water run-off and drainage upon the Sideyard Easement that results in erosion of the surface thereof;

and PROVIDED, FURTHER, that the owner of the Servient Estate shall not construct, install or otherwise cause to be made any door, window, duct, vent or aperture of any kind in any wall, fence of other structure on the Servient Estate which abuts or adjoins the Sideyard Easement.

Exhibit B

Conditions and Restrictions with Respect to Fences and Walls

1. Any fence or wall located along or about any boundary line of the lot subject hereto, which fence or wall is part of the instant conveyance of the subject premises to the Grantee, shall be maintained in good condition and repair by the Grantee and shall not be removed, replaced, destroyed or materially altered by the Grantee except upon mutual agreement of the Grantee and the owner or owners whose adjoining lot or lots are physically separated from the lot subject hereto by such fence or wall; and the cost and expense of maintaining any such fence or wall shall be shared equally by the Grantee and such adjoining owner or owners.

2. Any fence or wall located on the lot subject hereto, which fence or wall abuts or adjoins a Sideyard Easement to which the lot subject hereto may also be subject, as defined and described in the preceding Exhibit "A", and which fence or wall is part of the instant conveyance of the subject premises to the Grantee, shall be maintained in good condition and repair by the Grantee and shall not be moved, replaced, destroyed or materially altered by the Grantee except upon mutual agreement of the Grantee and the owner or owners of the adjoining lot to which the aforesaid Sideyard Easement is appurtenant.

3. Any fence or wall or portion thereof located upon a Sideyard Easement over and across an adjoining lot, as defined and described in the preceding Exhibit "A", which fence or wall or portion thereof is part of the instant conveyance of the subject premises to the Grantee, shall be maintained in good condition and repair by the Grantee and shall not be moved, replaced, destroyed or materially altered by the Grantee and the owner or owners of the adjoining lot subject to the aforesaid Sideyard Easement.

End of Exhibit B

Appendix B

Department of Development Services
Huntington Beach, California

Ordinance Code
Low Density Residential Districts
R1 District

S. 9103   YARD REQUIREMENTS

All yards shall be measured from the existing or from the ultimate right-of-way lines as required by Article 973. (495-5/46, 556-1/50, 1077-8/64, 1705-1/50, 2166-2/77)

S. 9103.2.1.1   EXCEPTION. ZERO SIDE YARD.

The side yard setback may be zero on one side of the lot provided that:

(a) The lot adjacent to that side yard is held under the same ownership at the time of initial construction and the minimum side yard setback for such adjacent lot is either zero or not less than (10) feet; and

(b) The opposite side yard setback is not less than ten (10) feet and is perpetually maintained free and clear from any obstructions other than a three (3) foot eave encroachment; swimming pools, normal landscaping; removable patio covers which extend to and not more than five (5) feet of the side property line; or garden walls or fences crossing said setback provided they are equipped with a gate, and may be equal in height to first floor double plate but not exceeding nine (9) feet; and

(c) The wall located at the zero side yard setback is constructed with maintenance-free, solid decorative masonry for the first story of the dwelling and the second story is constructed with maintenance-free, decorative masonry or masonry veneer with a minimum thickness of two (2) inches. Decorative construction need not be used on that portion of the structure obscured from the vision of the adjacent side yard by the wall located at the zero side yard setback. The wall so constructed shall intersect rear property lines; and

(d) No portion of the dwelling or architectural features project over any property line; and

(e) The dwelling is not constructed in accordance with the rear yard setback exception allowed in Section 9103.3.1.1; and

(f) The zero side yard is not adjacent to a public or private right-of-way; and

(g) Exposure protection between structures is provided according to the specifications of the Huntington Beach Fire Department and Huntington Beach Department of Building and Safety; and

(h) An administrative review application, accompanied by a precise plan, is submitted to the Board of Zoning Adjustments and approved or conditionally approved by the Board prior to issuance of building permits for the dwelling. Said plan shall delineate all structures proposed for initial construction. The Board, after reviewing said matter, may approve, conditionally approve or deny the precise plan. In its review the Board shall consider placement of all structures, building material and finishing of the wall constructed along the side lot line. (1469-2/69)

S. 9103.3.1   EXCEPTION. ZERO REAR YARD SETBACK.

The rear yard setback may be reduced to zero provided that:

(a) The lot adjacent to that rear yard is held under the same ownership at the time of initial construction, and the minimum rear yard setback for such adjacent lot is either zero or not less than ten (10) feet; and

(b) The wall located at the zero rear yard setback is constructed with maintenance-free, solid decorative masonry for the first story of the dwelling and the second story is constructed with maintenance-free, decorative masonry or masonry veneer with a minimum thickness of two (2) inches. Decorative construction need not be used on that portion of the structure obscured from the vision of the adjacent rear yard by the wall located at the zero rear yard setback. The wall so constructed shall intersect side property lines; and

(c) No portion of the dwelling or architectural features project over any property lines; and

(d) The dwelling is not constructed in accordance with the side yard setback exception allowed by Section 9103.2.1.1; and

(e) The zero rear yard is not adjacent to a public or private right-of-way; and

(f) Exposure protection between structures is provided according to the specifications of the Huntington Beach Fire Department and the Huntington Beach Department of Building and Safety; and

(g) An administrative review application, accompanied by a precise plan, is submitted to the Board of Zoning Adjustments and approved or conditionally approved by the Board prior to issuance of building permits for the dwelling. Said plan shall delineate all structures proposed for initial construction. The Board, after reviewing said matter, may approve, conditionally approve or deny the precise plan. In its review the Board shall consider placement of all structures, building material and finishing of the wall constructed along the rear lot line. (1469-2/69)

Oldtown Specific District

S. 9156 DEVELOPMENT STANDARDS. GENERAL
S.9156.4 SETBACKS

(a) Main Buildings

(2) Side Yard Setback: Except as provided herein, the aggregate setback shall be not less than twenty (20) percent of the site frontage and a minimum of three (3) feet shall be provided in each side yard.

(i) Any side yard abutting a public street shall have a setback of not less than five (5) feet, except for garages located on a single, twenty-five (25) foot lot, said setback may be reduced to not less than three (3) feet.

(ii) *Any side yard not abutting an arterial or local street may be reduced to zero* provided that the side yard area reduced by this procedure is made up on the opposite side yard of the site. Further provided, where zero side yard setback is used, the abutting side must be held under the abutting properties record agreement or deed restriction and consent in writing to such zero setback. A separation of not less than five (5) feet shall be provided between facing structures on abutting sites where zero side setback is utilized. This requirement shall not apply where the same interior property line is utilized for zero side yard construction on both sites.

(iii) Further provided, where the main entry to a dwelling is taken from a side yard area, said area abutting the main entry shall be not less than five (5) feet for the first story.

(b) Accessory Buildings

(2) Minimum Side Yard Setback: Except as provided herein, the aggregate setback shall be not less than [twenty (20)] percent of the site frontage and a minimum of three (3) feet shall be provided in each side yard.

(i) Any side yard abutting a public street shall have a setback of not less than five (5) feet, except for garages located on a single, twenty-five (25) foot lot, said setback may be reduced to not less than three (3) feet.

(ii) Any side yard not abutting an arterial or local street may be reduced to zero provided that the side yard area reduced by this procedure is made up on the opposite side yard of the site. Further provided where zero sideyard setback is used, the abutting site must be held under the same ownership at the same time of initial construction or the owners of the abutting properties record agreement or deed restriction and consent in writing to such zero setback. A separation of not less than five (5) feet shall be provided between facing structures on abutting sites where zero side setback is utilized. This requirement shall not apply where the same interior property line is utilized for zero side yard construction on both sites.

Low Residential District
R2 District

S. 9163 YARD REQUIREMENTS
S. 9163.2.1.1 EXCEPTION. ZERO SIDE YARD.

The side yard setback may be zero on one side of the lot provided that:

(a) The lot adjacent to that side yard is held under the same ownership at the time of initial construction and the mininum side yard setback for such adjacent lot is either zero or not less than ten (10) feet; and

(b) The opposite side yard setback is not less than ten (10) feet and is perpetually maintained free and clear from any obstructions other than a three (3) foot eave encroachment; swimming pools, normal landscaping; removable patio covers which may extend to and not more than five (5) feet of the side property line; or garden walls or fences crossing said setback provided they are equipped with a gate, and may be equal in height to first floor double plate but not exceeding nine (9) feet; and

(c) The wall located at the zero side yard setback is constructed with maintenance-free solid decorative masonry for the first story of the dwelling and the second story is constructed with maintenance-free, decorative masonry or masonry veneer with a minimum thickness of two (2) inches. Decorative construction need not be used on that portion of the structure obscured from the vision of the adjacent side yard by the wall located at the zero side yard setback. The wall so constructed shall intersect rear property lines; and

(d) No portion of the dwelling or architectural features project over any property line; and

(e) The dwelling is not constructed in accordance with the rear yard setback exception allowed in Section 9163.3.1; and

(f) The zero side yard is not adjacent to a public or private right-of-way; and

(g) Exposure protection between structures is provided according to the specifications of the Huntington Beach Fire Department and Huntington Beach Department of Building and Safety; and

(h) An administrative review application, accompanied by a precise plan is submitted to the Board of Zoning Adjustments and approved or conditionally approved by the Board prior to issuance of building permits for the dwelling. Said plan shall delineate all structures proposed for initial construction. The Board, after reviewing said matter, may approve, conditionally approve or deny the precise plan. In its review, the Board shall consider placement of all structures, building material and finishing of the wall constructed along the side lot line. (1469)

S. 9163.3.1 EXCEPTION. ZERO REAR YARD SETBACK.

The rear yard setback may be reduced to zero provided that:

(a) The lot adjacent to that side yard is held under the same ownership at the time of initial construction and the minimum side yard setback for such adjacent lot is either zero or not less than ten (10) feet; and

(b) The wall located at the zero side yard setback is constructed with maintenance-free solid decorative masonry for the first story of the dwelling and the second story is constructed with maintenance-free, decorative masonry or masonry veneer with a minimum thickness of two (2) inches. Decorative construction need not be used on that portion of the structure obscured from the vision of the adjacent side yard by the wall located at the zero side yard setback. The wall so constructed shall intersect rear property lines; and

(c) No portion of the dwelling or architectural features project over any property line; and

(d) The dwelling is not constructed in accordance with the rear yard setback exception allowed in Section 9163.3.1; and

(e) The zero rear yard is not adjacent to a public or private right-of-way; and

(f) Exposure protection between structures is provided according to the specifications of the Huntington Beach Fire Department and Huntington Beach Department of Building and Safety; and

(g) An administrative review application, accompanied by a precise plan, is submitted to the Board of Zoning Adjustments and approved or conditionally approved by the Board prior to issuance of building permits for the dwelling. Said plan shall delineate all structures proposed for initial construction. The Board, after reviewing said matter, may approve, conditionally approve or deny the precise plan. In its review, the Board shall consider placement of all structures, building material and finishing of the wall constructed along the side lot line. (1469)

High Density Residential Districts
R3 District

S. 9203 YARD REQUIREMENTS

S. 9203.2.1.1 EXCEPTION. ZERO SIDE YARD.

The side yard setback may be zero on one side of the lot provided that:

(a) The lot adjacent to that side yard is held under the same ownership at the time of initial construction and the minimum side yard setback for such adjacent lot is either zero or not less than ten (10) feet; and

(b) The opposite side yard setback is not less than ten (10) feet and is perpetually maintained free and clear from any obstructions other than a three (3) foot eave encroachment; swimming pools, normal landscaping; removable patio covers which may extend to and not more than five (5) feet of the side property line; or garden walls or fences crossing said setback provided they are equipped with a gate, and may be equal in height to first floor double plate but not exceeding nine (9) feet; and

(c) The wall located at the zero side yard setback is constructed with maintenance-free solid decorative masonry for the first story of the dwelling and the second story is constructed with maintenance-free, decorative masonry or masonry veneer with a minimum thickness of two (2) inches. Decorative construction need not be used on that portion of the structure obscured from the vision of the adjacent side yard by the wall located at the zero side yard setback. The wall so constructed shall intersect rear property lines; and

(d) No portion of the dwelling or architectural features project over any property line; and

(e) The dwelling is not constructed in accordance with the rear yard setback exception allowed in Section 9163.3.1; and

(f) The zero side yard is not adjacent to a public or private right-of-way; and

(g) Exposure protection between structures is provided according to the specifications of the Huntington Beach Fire Department and Huntington Beach Department of Building and Safety; and

(h) An administrative review application, accompanied by a precise plan, is submitted to the Board of Zoning Adjustments and approved or conditionally approved by the Board prior to issuance of building permits for the dwelling. Said plan shall delineate all structures proposed for initial construction. The Board, after reviewing said matter, may approve, conditionally approve or deny the precise plan. In its review, the Board shall consider placement of all structures, building material and finishing of the wall constructed along the side lot line. (1469)

S. 9203.3.1 EXCEPTION. ZERO REAR YARD SETBACK.

The rear yard setback may be reduced to zero provided that:

(a) The lot adjacent to that side yard is held under the same ownership at the time of initial construction and the minimum side yard setback for such adjacent lot is either zero or not less than ten (10) feet; and

(b) The wall located at the zero side yard setback is constructed with maintenance-free solid decorative masonry for the first story of the dwelling and the second story is constructed with maintenance-free, decorative masonry or masonry veneer with a minimum thickness of two (2) inches. Decorative construction need not be used on that portion of the structure obscured from the vision of the adjacent side yard by the wall located at the zero side yard setback. The wall so constructed shall intersect rear property lines; and

(c) No portion of the dwelling or architectural features project over any property line; and

(d) The dwelling is not constructed in accordance with the rear yard setback exception allowed in Section 9163.3.1; and

(e) The zero rear yard is not adjacent to a public or private right-of-way; and

(f) Exposure protection between structures is provided according to the specifications of the Huntington Beach Fire Department and Huntington Beach Department of Building and Safety; and

(g) An administrative review application, accompanied by a precise plan, is submitted to the Board of Zoning Adjustments and approved or conditionally approved by the Board prior to issuance of building permits for the dwelling. Said plan shall delineate all structures proposed for initial construction. The Board, after reviewing said matter, may approve, conditionally approve or deny the precise plan. In its review, the Board shall consider placement of all structures, building material and finishing of the wall constructed along the side lot line. (1469)

R4 District

S. 9233 YARD REQUIREMENTS

S. 9233.2.1 EXCEPTION. ZERO SIDE YARD.

The side yard setback may be zero on one side of the lot provided that:

(a) The lot adjacent to that side yard is held under the same ownership at the time of initial construction and the minimum side yard setback for such adjacent lot is either zero or not less than ten (10) feet; and

(b) The opposite side yard setback is not less than ten (10) feet and is perpetually maintained free and clear from any obstructions other than a three (3) foot eave encroachment; swimming pools, normal landscaping; removable patio covers which may extend to and not more than five (5) feet of the side property line; or garden walls or fences crossing said setback provided they are equipped with a gate, and may be equal in height to first floor double plate but not exceeding nine (9) feet; and

(c) The wall located at the zero side yard setback is constructed with maintenance-free solid decorative masonry for the first story of the dwelling and the second story is constructed with maintenance-free, decorative masonry or masonry veneer with a minimum thickness of two (2) inches. Decorative construction need not be used on that portion of the structure obscured from the vision of the adjacent side yard by the wall located at the zero side yard setback. The wall so constructed shall intersect rear property lines; and

(d) No portion of the dwelling or architectural features project over any property line; and

(e) The dwelling is not constructed in accordance with the rear yard setback exception allowed in Section 9163.3.1; and

(f) The zero side yard is not adjacent to a public or private right-of-way; and

(g) Exposure protection between structures is provided according to the specifications of the Huntington Beach Fire Department and Huntington Beach Department of Building and Safety; and

(h) An administrative review application, accompanied by a precise plan, is submitted to the Board of Zon-
ing Adjustments and approved or conditionally approved by the Board prior to issuance of building permits for the dwelling. Said plan shall delineate all structures proposed for initial construction. The Board, after reviewing said matter, may approve, conditionally approve or deny the precise plan. In its review, the Board shall consider placement of all structures, building material and finishing of the wall constructed along the side lot line. (1469)

S. 9233.3.1 EXCEPTION. ZERO REAR YARD SETBACK.

The rear yard setback may be reduced to zero provided that:

(a) The lot adjacent to that side yard is held under the same ownership at the time of initial construction and the minimum side yard setback for such adjacent lot is either zero or not less than ten (10) feet; and

(b) The wall located at the zero side yard setback is constructed with maintenance-free solid decorative masonry for the first story of the dwelling and the second story is constructed with maintenance-free, decorative masonry or masonry veneer with a minimum thickness of two (2) inches. Decorative construction need not be used on that portion of the structure obscured from the vision of the adjacent side yard by the wall located at the zero side yard setback. The wall so constructed shall intersect rear property lines; and

(c) No portion of the dwelling or architectural features project over any property line; and

(d) The dwelling is not constructed in accordance with the rear yard setback exception allowed in Section 9163.3.1; and

(e) The zero rear yard is not adjacent to a public or private right-of-way; and

(f) Exposure protection between structures is provided according to the specifications of the Huntington Beach Fire Department and Huntington Beach Department of Building and Safety; and

(g) An administrative review application, accompanied by a precise plan, is submitted to the Board of Zoning Adjustments and approved or conditionally approved by the Board prior to issuance of building permits for the dwelling. Said plan shall delineate all structures proposed for initial construction. The Board, after reviewing said matter, may approve, conditionally approve or deny the precise plan. In its review, the Board shall consider placement of all structures, building material and finishing of the wall constructed along the side lot line. (1469)

Appendix C

Development Concept
Planning Form

HOH Associates, Inc.

DEVELOPMENT: Pradera
LOCATION: Boca Raton, Florida

DEVELOPER: Showcase Development, Ltd.

DATE: 8/27/80

DATE OPENED: 6/80
DATE FINISHED: In progress

HOUSING CONCEPT: Zero Lot Line
DENSITY: 5 du/ac
% OPEN SPACE:
ORGANIZATION OF OPEN SPACE: HOA

ZONING:
SETBACKS: 15'F; 0'S with 10' Bldg. sep.
PROJECT SIZE: 150 du; 30 ac.
LOT SIZES: 50 x 100

PLAN #/NAME	(1) Oleander	(2) Jasmine	(3) Gibiscus	(4) Gardenia
PRICE:	$132,900*	$137,900*	$146,900*	$144,900*
SQUARE FEET:	1460	1666	1920	1944
# OF LEVELS	1	1	1	1
BEDROOMS	1 + den	2	2 + den	3
BATHS	2	2	2	2
GARAGE	2-car	2-car	2-car	2-car
PLAN MIX	Random depending on buyer			
# SOLD	3	10	4	12

*Premium price on some lots

PHYSICAL CHARACTER:

EXTERIOR:
ROOF: clay barrel tile
SIDING: stucco
DRIVEWAY: concrete
FENCING: block with stucco and wrought iron
LANDSCAPING: included (front area in grass)
SPRINKLERS: yes, automatic
ARCH. TYPE: Mediterranean
COLORS: soft cream with red tile

PLANNING FEATURES:
PARKING: Planned islands w/ parking
STREET LAYOUT: Cul de sacs
STREET WIDTHS: 32' and 50' ROW
SPECIAL FEATURES: islands, lake lots, canal frontage
INNOVATIONS: monitored security
ENTRY: guard gate
COMMON AREAS: lake, island, pool, park.
IMAGE: quality, selective
BUILDING SEPARATIONS: 10'
ENERGY FEATURES:

Pradera

HOMEOWNERS ASSOCIATION: Yes

MONTHLY ASSESSMENT: $45.00
RECREATION FEE: No

INCLUDES:
o CLUBHOUSE/REC. ROOM
● SWIMMING POOL (#)
o TENNIS COURTS (#)
o JACUZZI (#)
o SAUNA (#)
● BIKEPATHS
● FIELD GAMES
● OTHER Lake-boating, fishing

o MAINTENANCE OF EXTERIOR
o INSURANCE
o WATER
● MAINT. COMMON SPACE
● OTHER: Front yards, boulevards
Lake area, Park area
Perimeter Wall area, Security house
Pool area

BUYER PROFILE:
Average Age: 45-50
# of Children: minimal
Average Income: $50,000 +

Prev. Residence: 50% out of state / 50% local
Both Spouses Work: No
Occupation Category: Executives/ Business owners

FINANCING OFFERED:
o FHA
o VA

● CONVENTIONAL
● OTHER

SALES PROFILE AND HISTORY:
Date Opened: 6/80
Weekly Sales Rate: desire 8/mo

Sold to Date: 29
Total Unsold: 42

MATERIALS TO OBTAIN:
● Sales Brochure
● Price List
● Floor Plans
● Deed Restrictions
o Covenants

● Photographs
● Site Plan
o Approved Development Plan
● HOA Documents

INTERVIEWER: David R. Jensen

Development Concept
Planning Form

DEVELOPMENT: Patio Homes at Cypress   DATE: 8/27/80
LOCATION: Boca West
             Boca Raton, Point, Florida   DATE OPENED: 11/80
DEVELOPER: National Building and Devel. Corp DATE FINISHED: __

HOUSING CONCEPT: Zero Lot Line   ZONING: PUD
DENSITY: 4.3   SETBACKS: F:Zero; S:7½; B:10'
% OPEN SPACE: None   PROJECT SIZE: 4.1 ac, 18 lots
ORGANIZATION OF OPEN SPACE: HOA with Master LOT SIZES: 60 x 105

---

	(1)	(2)	(3)	(4)
PLAN #/NAME				
PRICE:	$325,000	$375,000		
SQUARE FEET:	3000 SF	3400 SF		
			Isaac Scklar, Architect	
# OF LEVELS	1	2		
BEDROOMS	3	4		
BATHS	2½	3		
GARAGE	2-car	2-car		

PLAN MIX
SOLD

PHYSICAL CHARACTER:

EXTERIOR: PLANNING FEATURES:
  ROOF: Cedar shake   PARKING: 2-car side entry
  SIDING: stucco   STREET LAYOUT: cul de sac
  DRIVEWAY: exposed aggregated   STREET WIDTHS: 60' ROW; 22'
  FENCING: Stucco Wall   SPECIAL FEATURES: pavement
  LANDSCAPING: $6000/min.   INNOVATIONS:
  SPRINKLERS: yes   ENTRY: Village identification
  ARCH. TYPE: Pavilion (in pods)   COMMON AREAS: No
  COLORS: Beige and cedar   IMAGE: Hi Value, exclusive
                                         BUILDING SEPARATIONS: 7½'/floor
                                         ENERGY FEATURES: none

Patio Homes at Cypress
HOMEOWNERS ASSOCIATION: MONTHLY ASSESSMENT: $110.00
                                          RECREATION FEE: No

INCLUDES:
  o CLUBHOUSE/REC. ROOM   ● MAINTENANCE OF EXTERIOR
  o SWIMMING POOL (#)   Separate Club ● INSURANCE
  o TENNIS COURTS (#)   membership only ● WATER
  o JACUZZI (#)   ● MAINT. COMMON SPACE
  o SAUNA (#)   ● OTHER:
  o BIKEPATHS
  o FIELD GAMES   Landscape maintenance
  o OTHER

BUYER PROFILE: 30% primary; 70% secondary
Average Age: 55   Prev. Residence: out-of-state
# of Children 2½   Both Spouses Work: No
Average Income: $100,000+   Occupation Category: Executive

FINANCING OFFERED:
  o FHA   ● CONVENTIONAL 70%
  o VA   ● OTHER 30% cash

SALES PROFILE AND HISTORY:
Date Opened: Nov. 1980   # Sold to Date: ____
Weekly Sales Rate: -----   Total Unsold: _____

MATERIALS TO OBTAIN:
  o Sales Brochure   o Photographs
  o Price List   o Site Plan
  o Floor Plans   o Approved Development Plan
  o Deed Restrictions   o HOA Documents
  o Covenants

                    INTERVIEWER: David R. Jensen

Development Concept
Planning Form

DEVELOPMENT: Turtle Rock Ridge
LOCATION: Irvine, CA

DEVELOPER: Irvine Pacific

DATE: 7/80

DATE OPENED: 1/80
DATE FINISHED:

HOUSING CONCEPT: Detached, Zero Lot Line
DENSITY: 4.9 du/ac
% OPEN SPACE: 100 acres in Master Area of 250 ac.
ORGANIZATION OF OPEN SPACE: Deeded to the City

ZONING: front min 5'
SETBACKS: none between 5-18'
PROJECT SIZE: 110 units/27.3 ac.
LOT SIZES: 50 x 100

PLAN #/NAME	(1) TRV-B1	(2) TRV-B2	(3) TRV-B3	(4)
PRICE:	$175,000	$215,000	$230,000	
SQUARE FEET:	1,915	2,698	2,882	
# OF LEVELS	1	2	2	
BEDROOMS	2+1	3+1	4	
BATHS	2	3	2½	
GARAGE	2-car	3-car	3-car	
PLAN MIX	30%	35%	35%	
# SOLD				

PHYSICAL CHARACTER:

EXTERIOR:
 ROOF: shake
 SIDING: stucco
 DRIVEWAY: concrete
 FENCING: slurry stone and wood
 LANDSCAPING: not included
 SPRINKLERS:
 ARCH. TYPE: California contemp.
 COLORS: earth tone

PLANNING FEATURES:
 PARKING:
 STREET LAYOUT: cul de sac and loop
 STREET WIDTHS: 46' ROW
 SPECIAL FEATURES:
 INNOVATIONS: 3000 SF house on 5000
                              SF lot
 ENTRY:
 COMMON AREAS:
 IMAGE:
 BUILDING SEPARATIONS:
 ENERGY FEATURES:

Turtle Rock Ridge

HOMEOWNERS ASSOCIATION:

MONTHLY ASSESSMENT: $32.00
RECREATION FEE:

INCLUDES:
 ● CLUBHOUSE/REC. ROOM Master Assn.
 ● SWIMMING POOL (#) 1/400 du.
 ● TENNIS COURTS (#) 2/400 du.
 ● JACUZZI (#)
 o SAUNA (#)
 ● BIKEPATHS
 o FIELD GAMES
 ● OTHER   Community Park
              Pedestrian paths

 o MAINTENANCE OF EXTERIOR
 o INSURANCE
 o WATER
 o MAINT. COMMON SPACE
 o OTHER:

BUYER PROFILE:
Average Age: 35-50
# of Children 15-1.8   10 years and up
Average Income: $50,000 +

Prev. Residence: Irvine (move up)
Both Spouses Work: prevalent
Occupation Category: Admin., mgt, etc.

FINANCING OFFERED:
 o FHA
 o VA

 ● CONVENTIONAL
 o OTHER

SALES PROFILE AND HISTORY:
Date Opened: 1/80
Weekly Sales Rate: 1.3

Sold to Date:
Total Unsold:

MATERIALS TO OBTAIN:
 ● Sales Brochure
 o Price List
 o Floor Plans
 o Deed Restrictions
 o Covenants

 o Photographs
 ● Site Plan
 ● Approved Development Plan
 ● HOA Documents

INTERVIEWER: David R. Jensen

Development Concept
Planning Form

DEVELOPMENT: Paseo Verde of Rock Creek
LOCATION: Hollywood, Florida
DEVELOPER: Hollywood, Inc.

DATE: 8/28/80
DATE OPENED: 4/79
DATE FINISHED: 8/79

HOUSING CONCEPT: Zero Lot Line Patio House
DENSITY: 7 du/ac
% OPEN SPACE:
ORGANIZATION OF OPEN SPACE:

ZONING: PUD (MF)
SETBACKS: none
PROJECT SIZE: 80 du/12ac
LOT SIZES: 85' x 65'

PLAN #/NAME	(1)	(2)	(3)	(4)
PRICE:	$59,990	$56,990	$66,990	$75,990
SQUARE FEET:	1,544	1,439	1,679	1,890
# OF LEVELS	1	1	1	2
BEDROOMS	3	3	3	4
BATHS	2	2	2	3
GARAGE	2-car	2-car	2-car	2-car
PLAN MIX	30%	20%	30%	20%
# SOLD	24	16	24	16

PHYSICAL CHARACTER:

EXTERIOR:
ROOF: asphalt
SIDING: stucco and plywood on upper levels
DRIVEWAY: asphalt
FENCING: vertical wood cedar
LANDSCAPING: yes
SPRINKLERS: yes
ARCH. TYPE: Spanish
COLORS: earth

PLANNING FEATURES:
PARKING: 2 gar./2 drive
STREET LAYOUT: loop and culs
STREET WIDTHS: 20'
SPECIAL FEATURES: enclosed front yard
INNOVATIONS: narrow streets
ENTRY:
COMMON AREAS:
IMAGE:
BUILDING SEPARATIONS: 7½
ENERGY FEATURES:

Paseo Verde of Rock Creek
HOMEOWNERS ASSOCIATION:

MONTHLY ASSESSMENT: $15.00
RECREATION FEE: $300.00/yr
                    private

INCLUDES:
o CLUBHOUSE/REC. ROOM
o SWIMMING POOL (#)
o TENNIS COURTS (#)
o JACUZZI (#)
o SAUNA (#)
● BIKEPATHS
● FIELD GAMES
● OTHER Lake, boating, pocket parks

o MAINTENANCE OF EXTERIOR
o INSURANCE
o WATER
● MAINT. COMMON SPACE
● OTHER: Lakes, Street lights

This project is part of a larger one that provides a major club, lake, recreation and marketing image.

BUYER PROFILE:
Average Age: 35-40
# of Children 2
Average Income: $25-30,000

Prev. Residence: Dade County
Both Spouses Work: In many instances
Occupation Category: Young Profs., managerial, etc.

FINANCING OFFERED:
o FHA
o VA

● CONVENTIONAL 80%
● OTHER cash

SALES PROFILE AND HISTORY:
Date Opened: 4/79
Weekly Sales Rate:

Sold to Date: 80
Total Unsold: None

MATERIALS TO OBTAIN:
o Sales Brochure
o Price List
o Floor Plans
o Deed Restrictions
o Covenants

● Photographs
● Site Plan
o Approved Development Plan
● HOA Documents C and RS

INTERVIEWER: David R. Jensen

HOH Associates, Inc.

DEVELOPMENT: Wood Creek Courts
LOCATION: Lincolnshire, Ill.

DATE: 9/11/80

DEVELOPER: Blietz Organization

DATE OPENED: 1972
DATE FINISHED: 1978

HOUSING CONCEPT: SF detached - adult
DENSITY: 3.6 du/ac
% OPEN SPACE:
ORGANIZATION OF OPEN SPACE: Woods and lakes

ZONING:
SETBACKS:
PROJECT SIZE: 20.18
LOT SIZES: 5000 (50 x 100)

	(1)	(2)	(3)	(4)
PLAN #/NAME	3 models		1980 resale	
PRICE:	100,000		135,900	
SQUARE FEET:	1760	2200	2400	
# OF LEVELS	Ranch	2 + basement	2 + basement	
BEDROOMS	3	3	3	
BATHS	2½	2½	2½	
GARAGE	2½-car	2½-car	2½-car	
PLAN MIX	1/3	1/3	1/3	
# SOLD	Project is sold out			

PHYSICAL CHARACTER:

EXTERIOR:
 ROOF: Cedar shakes
 SIDING: Frame construction, brick, veneer stone, cedar
 DRIVEWAY: Asphalt
 FENCING: Masonry/wrought iron/plain cedar
 LANDSCAPING: Yes 5000/du
 SPRINKLERS: ----------
 ARCH. TYPE: varying early American
 COLORS: Earth

PLANNING FEATURES:
 PARKING: Gar. and drive. and culs
 STREET LAYOUT: loop and culs.
 STREET WIDTHS: all private
 SPECIAL FEATURES: trees
 INNOVATIONS: Zero Lot line
 ENTRY:
 COMMON AREAS:
 IMAGE: Positive
 BUILDING SEPARATIONS:
 ENERGY FEATURES:

Wood Creek Courts
HOMEOWNERS ASSOCIATION:

MONTHLY ASSESSMENT: $93 in 1978
RECREATION FEE: $125 in 1980

INCLUDES:
 o CLUBHOUSE/REC. ROOM
 o SWIMMING POOL (#)
 o TENNIS COURTS (#)
 o JACUZZI (#)
 o SAUNA (#)
 o BIKEPATHS
 o FIELD GAMES
 o OTHER

 ● MAINTENANCE OF EXTERIOR
 o INSURANCE
 o WATER
 o MAINT. COMMON SPACE
 o OTHER:
 ponds and lakes
 forests

BUYER PROFILE:
Average Age: 50 +
# of Children 0-1
Average Income: $100,000 +

Prev. Residence: Metro Area
Both Spouses Work: -----
Occupation Category: Corp. Execs.

FINANCING OFFERED:
 o FHA
 o VA

 o CONVENTIONAL
 o OTHER

SALES PROFILE AND HISTORY:
Date Opened: 1972
Weekly Sales Rate:

Sold to Date:
Total Unsold:

MATERIALS TO OBTAIN:
 o Sales Brochure
 o Price List
 o Floor Plans
 o Deed Restrictions
 ● Covenants

 ● Photographs
 ● Site Plan
 ● Approved Development Plan
 o HOA Documents

INTERVIEWER: David R. Jensen

HOH Associates, Inc.

DEVELOPMENT: Montiel Patio Homes
LOCATION: Mission Viejo, CA

DEVELOPER: Mission Viejo Company

DATE: 4/80

DATE OPENED: 5/14/77
DATE FINISHED:

Modified
HOUSING CONCEPT: Zero Lot Line with 3' and 7'
DENSITY: 4-5 du/ac.   easements
% OPEN SPACE:
ORGANIZATION OF OPEN SPACE:

ZONING:
SETBACKS: front 20' to sidewalk
PROJECT SIZE: 681 units
LOT SIZES: 50 x 100

PLAN #/NAME	(1) A	(2) B	(3) C	(4) D	(5) E
PRICE:	$107,065	$110,785	$117,655	$128,790	$132,790
SQUARE FEET:	1,225	1,373	1,560	1,868	2,033
# OF LEVELS	1	1	1	2	2
BEDROOMS	2+1	2+1	2+1	4	4
BATHS	2	2	2	3	2½
GARAGE	2-car	2-car	2-car	2-car	2-car
PLAN MIX	61	90	142	191	184
# SOLD	57	83	122	180	180

PHYSICAL CHARACTER:

EXTERIOR:
  ROOF: wood shingle
  SIDING: stucco
  DRIVEWAY: concrete
  FENCING: not included
  LANDSCAPING: not included
  SPRINKLERS: not included
  ARCH. TYPE: Spanish
  COLORS: earth tone

PLANNING FEATURES:
  PARKING: 4/each lot
  STREET LAYOUT:
  STREET WIDTHS: { 56' collector / 52' local / 48' local / 40' local
  SPECIAL FEATURES:
  INNOVATIONS:
  ENTRY:
  COMMON AREAS:
  IMAGE:
  BUILDING SEPARATIONS:
  ENERGY FEATURES:

Montiel Patio Homes
HOMEOWNERS ASSOCIATION:
    Lake Mission Viejo Assn.

MONTHLY ASSESSMENT: $8.50
RECREATION FEE: $22/mo.
Slope and landscape maint. $29.00

INCLUDES:
o CLUBHOUSE/REC. ROOM
o SWIMMING POOL (#)
o TENNIS COURTS (#)
o JACUZZI (#)
o SAUNA (#)
o BIKEPATHS
o FIELD GAMES
● OTHER   County Park

Not included
in parcels.
Membership in community
Recreation

o MAINTENANCE OF EXTERIOR
o INSURANCE
o WATER
● MAINT. COMMON SPACE (slopes within tract)
o OTHER:

BUYER PROFILE:
Average Age: 32
# of Children 0.8
Average Income: $40,000

Prev. Residence:
Both Spouses Work:
Occupation Category:

FINANCING OFFERED:
o FHA
o VA

● CONVENTIONAL
o OTHER

SALES PROFILE AND HISTORY:
Date Opened: 5/77
Weekly Sales Rate: 4.12

Sold to Date: 686
Total Unsold: 46

MATERIALS TO OBTAIN:
● Sales Brochure
o Price List
o Floor Plans
o Deed Restrictions
o Covenants

o Photographs
o Site Plan
o Approved Development Plan
● HOA Documents CC & R

INTERVIEWER: David R. Jensen

Development Concept
Planning Form

HOH Associates, Inc.

DEVELOPMENT: 4000 sq. ft.
LOCATION: Oahu, Hawaii

DATE:

DEVELOPER: Gentry Pacific, Ltd.

DATE OPENED: 7/78
DATE FINISHED:

HOUSING CONCEPT: Zero Lot Line
DENSITY: 8 du/ac
% OPEN SPACE:
ORGANIZATION OF OPEN SPACE:
    (100 planned - part of larger project)

ZONING:
SETBACKS:
PROJECT SIZE: 10-12 acres
LOT SIZES: 4000 sq. ft.

	(1)	(2)	(3)	(4)
PLAN #/NAME	4 models			
PRICE:	130,000-170,000			
SQUARE FEET:	1200-1950			
# OF LEVELS	1 and 2			
BEDROOMS	3 and 4			
BATHS	2 and 2½			
GARAGE	2-car			
PLAN MIX	Even			
# SOLD	250 total			

PHYSICAL CHARACTER:

EXTERIOR:
  ROOF:
  SIDING:
  DRIVEWAY:
  FENCING:
  LANDSCAPING:
  SPRINKLERS:
  ARCH. TYPE:
  COLORS:

PLANNING FEATURES:
  PARKING:
  STREET LAYOUT:
  STREET WIDTHS:
  SPECIAL FEATURES:
  INNOVATIONS:
  ENTRY:
  COMMON AREAS:
  IMAGE:
  BUILDING SEPARATIONS:
  ENERGY FEATURES:

4000 sq. ft.
Oahu, Hawaii
HOMEOWNERS ASSOCIATION:

MONTHLY ASSESSMENT: $50/yr.
RECREATION FEE:

INCLUDES:
  o CLUBHOUSE/REC. ROOM
  o SWIMMING POOL (#)
  o TENNIS COURTS (#)
  o JACUZZI (#)
  o SAUNA (#)
  o BIKEPATHS
  o FIELD GAMES
  o OTHER

  o MAINTENANCE OF EXTERIOR
  o INSURANCE
  o WATER
  o MAINT. COMMON SPACE
  o OTHER:

BUYER PROFILE:
Average Age: 35-40
# of Children 2
Average Income: $40,000

Prev. Residence: within 5 miles
Both Spouses Work: Yes
Occupation Category: All

FINANCING OFFERED:
  o FHA
  o VA

  ● CONVENTIONAL
  o OTHER

SALES PROFILE AND HISTORY:
Date Opened: 1978
Weekly Sales Rate:

Sold to Date: 250
Total Unsold:

MATERIALS TO OBTAIN:
  ● Sales Brochure
  o Price List
  o Floor Plans
  o Deed Restrictions
  ● Covenants

  o Photographs
  ● Site Plan
  o Approved Development Plan
  o HOA Documents

INTERVIEWER: David R. Jensen

126

Development Concept
Planning Form

HOH Associates, Inc.

DEVELOPMENT: Green Run
LOCATION: Green Run, Virginia Beach, VA
DEVELOPER: Green Run Development Corporation

DATE: November 3, 1980

DATE OPENED: 1970
DATE FINISHED: 1975

HOUSING CONCEPT: Zero Lot Line S.F.D.
DENSITY: 5 du/acre
% OPEN SPACE: Min Parcel O.S.
ORGANIZATION OF OPEN SPACE: Parks; Project-wide
   walkway easements in rear

ZONING: P.U.D. 5.2 du/ac Mar
SETBACKS: None Req./12' Min distance
   Btwn bldg
PROJECT SIZE: 10.5 ac/59du
LOT SIZES: 7 ac/23 du
   70' front, 100' depth

PLAN #/NAME	(1) Redwood	(2) Gold Coast	(3) Monterey	(4) Barbary
PRICE: (early '72)	32,900	37,900	36,900	35,900
SQUARE FEET:	1,695	2,383	2,332	2,105
# OF LEVELS	1	2½	2	1
BEDROOMS	3	4	4	4
BATHS	2	2½	3	2
GARAGE	2 car	2 car	2 car	2 car

PLAN MIX
SOLD
   Lot Price $14,000/lot   Conventional 80-90' $15,000/lot

PHYSICAL CHARACTER:

EXTERIOR:
   ROOF: Asphalt 5:12
   SIDING: Composition board w/ accent brick
   DRIVEWAY: 18' concrete
   FENCING: exterior grade plywood
   LANDSCAPING: modest
   SPRINKLERS: no
   ARCH. TYPE: Calif. contemporary
   COLORS: earth tones

PLANNING FEATURES:
   PARKING: 2 car garage + 2 on apron
   STREET LAYOUT: all cul-de-sacs
   STREET WIDTHS: 30' center to curb
   SPECIAL FEATURES: open cul ends
   INNOVATIONS: concentric street layout
      no sidewalks on street
   ENTRY:
   COMMON AREAS: Village wide easements
      in back
   IMAGE: clear surburban
   BUILDING SEPARATIONS: 15' - 20'
   ENERGY FEATURES: all electric

HOMEOWNERS ASSOCIATION: Mandatory Assoc.

MONTHLY ASSESSMENT: $11/mo
RECREATION FEE: (included)

INCLUDES:
   ● CLUBHOUSE/REC. ROOM (1) Pagoda + bathhouses
   ● SWIMMING POOL (# 3)
   ● TENNIS COURTS (# 6)
   o JACUZZI (#)
   o SAUNA (#)
   o BIKEPATHS
   ● FIELD GAMES (7 acres - Open field little league)
   ● OTHER (canal system)

   o MAINTENANCE OF EXTERIOR
   ● INSURANCE (except liability)
   o WATER
   ● MAINT. COMMON SPACE
   o OTHER:

BUYER PROFILE:
Average Age: early 30's
# of Children 2-3
Average Income: $15,000 - $20,000

Prev. Residence: West Coast
Both Spouses Work: No
Occupation Category: Military; Doctors;
   Professional

FINANCING OFFERED:
   ● FHA
   ● VA

   ● CONVENTIONAL
   o OTHER

SALES PROFILE AND HISTORY:
Date Opened:
Weekly Sales Rate:

Sold to Date:
Total Unsold:

MATERIALS TO OBTAIN:
   ● Sales Brochure
   ● Price List
   ● Floor Plans
   ● Deed Restrictions
   ● Covenants

   ● Photographs
   o Site Plan
   ● Approved Development Plan
   o HOA Documents

INTERVIEWER: Jay Parker

127

DEVELOPMENT: Red Oak
LOCATION: Farmington, Connecticut
Architect: Warren Callister
DEVELOPER: Otto Paparazzo Management, Inc.
Planner: Bill Walker

DATE: July 1980

DATE OPENED: August 25, 1980
DATE FINISHED: Estimated 3 years
Construction Start: December 13, 1979

multi-family

HOUSING CONCEPT: Attached unit/land lease
DENSITY: 277 units/65 acres + 7 acre park
% OPEN SPACE:
ORGANIZATION OF OPEN SPACE: Interior corridors
  adjacent to wooded park

ZONING: Residential Dev. Multiples
SETBACKS: none req.-By decision 27' EOP
PROJECT SIZE: 65 acre + 7 acre park
LOT SIZES: 30' x 130' avg.
Project Access: Public Loop Road
Dewlling Unit Access: Private Drives

	(1)	(2)	(3)	(4)
PLAN #/NAME	"Field House"	"Village House"	"Court House"	
PRICE:	$87,500/$65 month	$90,000/$65 month	$79,000/$65 month land lease	
SQUARE FEET:	1,925	2,280	1,820	
# OF LEVELS	3	3	2	
BEDROOMS	3	3	2	
BATHS	2	2	1½	
GARAGE	oversized single	oversized single	oversized single	

PLAN MIX: Predetermined (condition of zoning), problem - Court House
SOLD: very popular, most popular

PHYSICAL CHARACTER:

EXTERIOR:
  ROOF: ashpalt shingle
  SIDING: wood-stained
  DRIVEWAY: gravel/asphalt mix, very attractive,
    same $ as asphalt
  FENCING: included w/unit--individual for unit type
  LANDSCAPING: $1800/unit, extensive, lots of trees
  SPRINKLERS: none
  ARCH. TYPE: Traditional ext./Cont. Int.
  COLORS: pastel stains with contrasting trim

PLANNING FEATURES:
  PARKING: 2.3/unit, 1 oversized garage
  STREET LAYOUT: private cul-de-sacs
  STREET WIDTHS: 20' ±
  SPECIAL FEATURES: recreation pkg.
  INNOVATIONS: "leasehold" financing
  ENTRY: covered (wood) concrete porch
  COMMON AREAS:
  IMAGE: Exclusive, Very good!
  BUILDING SEPARATIONS: 35' (town req.)
  ENERGY FEATURES: elaborate insulation,
    lots of light, see brochure -
    "Design for Energy"

Red Oak

HOMEOWNERS ASSOCIATION:
  Winding Trails, Inc., 1 yr. mbrship.)
  Farmington Racquet Club, 2 yr. mbrship.) _____

INCLUDES:
  CLUBHOUSE/REC. ROOM
  o SWIMMING POOL (#)
  ● TENNIS COURTS (#2)
  o JACUZZI (#)
  o SAUNA (#)
  ● BIKEPATHS 7,000 l.f. of pathways
  o FIELD GAMES
  ● OTHER games, stocked lakes, skating
    basketball court

MONTHLY ASSESSMENT: $33
RECREATION FEE:
LAND LEASE: $65/yr.

  o MAINTENANCE OF EXTERIOR private roads & street lights
  o INSURANCE
  o WATER
  ● MAINT. COMMON SPACE
  o OTHER:

BUYER PROFILE:
Average Age: 35-40 (range 25-50)
# of Children: not many (some single heads-of-households)
Average Income: $45,000

Prev. Residence: within area/some local
Both Spouses Work: definitely
Occupation Category: Professional

FINANCING OFFERED:
  o FHA no
  o VA no (land lease)

Land lease concept must be explained to banks - 3
● CONVENTIONAL banks now work on loans.
  o OTHER

SALES PROFILE AND HISTORY:
Date Opened: July 25, 1980
Weekly Sales Rate: 2-4 (very new project)

Sold to Date: 18
Total Unsold: 8

MATERIALS TO OBTAIN:
  ● Sales Brochure
  ● Price List
  ● Floor Plans
  ● Deed Restrictions
  ● Covenants

  ● Photographs
  ● Site Plan
  ● Approved Development Plan
  o HOA Documents

INTERVIEWER: Jay Parker

Development Concept
Planning Form

HOH Associates, Inc.

DEVELOPMENT: Northwich
LOCATION: Brandermill, VA.
            (near Richmond)
DEVELOPER: Brandermill Group
  Franny Powell Dir. of Market and Public Relations

DATE: November 4, 1980

DATE OPENED: Late 77
DATE FINISHED: 6 months later
                (fastest selling lot)

HOUSING CONCEPT: Zero Lot Line Det. View Orient.
DENSITY:
% OPEN SPACE: (30% project wide)
ORGANIZATION OF OPEN SPACE:
        Along city Res.

ZONING: P.U.D. Condition use
SETBACKS: Side Yard - 2' from Zero
          Lot Line, 13' from other
          line.

PLAN #/NAME	(1)	(2)	(3)	(4)
PRICE:		Lots and homes		
SQUARE FEET:				
# OF LEVELS				
BEDROOMS				
BATHS				
GARAGE				
PLAN MIX				
# SOLD				

PHYSICAL CHARACTER:

EXTERIOR:
  ROOF:
  SIDING:
  DRIVEWAY:
  FENCING:
  LANDSCAPING:
  SPRINKLERS:
  ARCH. TYPE:
  COLORS:

PLANNING FEATURES:
  PARKING: 2 off Street spaces/units
  STREET LAYOUT: Curved Culs & loop
  STREET WIDTHS:
  SPECIAL FEATURES:
  INNOVATIONS: Country setting
  ENTRY:
  COMMON AREAS:
  IMAGE: Very woodsy/exclusive
  BUILDING SEPARATIONS: 15-17'
  ENERGY FEATURES:

SF Conv (Comp. View) 15-20,000 sq. ft. = $50,000 +/lot
SF Zero   = $25,000 +/lot

Northwich
HOMEOWNERS ASSOCIATION:

MONTHLY ASSESSMENT: $12/mo.
RECREATION FEE: Private club

INCLUDES:
- CLUBHOUSE/REC. ROOM Teen center
- SWIMMING POOL (#) (club)   800-1000'
- TENNIS COURTS (#) (club)
o JACUZZI (#)
o SAUNA (#)
- BIKEPATHS 15 miles
- FIELD GAMES
o OTHER

o MAINTENANCE OF EXTERIOR
o INSURANCE
o WATER
- MAINT. COMMON SPACE and streets
- OTHER:
  Priv. Country Club-
  Snow removal/swept weekly. Boating-
  Beach-Patrol-Boat rental
  Commercial Indoor tennis,
      racketball, nauticus

BUYER PROFILE:
Average Age: 27-35 and 50-65
# of Children 1- (2½ person households)
Average Income: 40,000

Active types
Prev. Residence: Richmond/or resale
                              Brandermill
Both Spouses Work: Not Likely. (30%)
Occupation Category:
                    Prof. Business

FINANCING OFFERED:
o FHA
o VA

- CONVENTIONAL
o OTHER
Lots- 15 year 10% 7 year balloon

SALES PROFILE AND HISTORY:
Date Opened: 1977
Weekly Sales Rate: 3/mo.

Sold to Date: 150
Total Unsold: 30 or 40 not developed
              or salable yet

MATERIALS TO OBTAIN:
- Sales Brochure
- Price List
o Floor Plans
- Deed Restrictions
- Covenants

o Photographs
- Site Plan
o Approved Development Plan
- HOA Documents

INTERVIEWER: Jay Parker

Selling single Zero Lot Line lots/Have to have view to sell/Real market hesitency
No builder seems to understand fencing/decks

Development Concept
Planning Form

HOH Associates, Inc.

DEVELOPMENT: Woodbridge Cottage Homes
LOCATION: Irvine, CA

DEVELOPER: Broadmoor Homes

DATE: 4/80

DATE OPENED:
DATE FINISHED:

Modified Zero Lot Line
HOUSING CONCEPT: patio yards
DENSITY: 8/acre
% OPEN SPACE: 10 %
ORGANIZATION OF OPEN SPACE: HOA

ZONING: R-1
SETBACKS: 10' from front
PROJECT SIZE: 268 total units
LOT SIZES: 30' x 80'

	(1)	(2)	(3)	(4)
PLAN #/NAME				
PRICE:	3 models			
SQUARE FEET:	93,000 - 120,000			
# OF LEVELS	1 and 2			
BEDROOMS	2 and 3			
BATHS	2 - 2½			
GARAGE	2-car standard			
PLAN MIX	15%	35%	50%	
# SOLD				

PHYSICAL CHARACTER:

EXTERIOR:
  ROOF:
  SIDING:
  DRIVEWAY: yes
  FENCING:
  LANDSCAPING:
  SPRINKLERS:
  ARCH. TYPE:
  COLORS:

PLANNING FEATURES:
  PARKING:
  STREET LAYOUT: grid
  STREET WIDTHS:
  SPECIAL FEATURES:
  INNOVATIONS: small lots, patio yards
  ENTRY:
  COMMON AREAS:
  IMAGE:
  BUILDING SEPARATIONS:
  ENERGY FEATURES:

Woodbridge Cottage Homes
HOMEOWNERS ASSOCIATION:

MONTHLY ASSESSMENT:
RECREATION FEE:

INCLUDES:
  o CLUBHOUSE/REC. ROOM
  o SWIMMING POOL (#)
  o TENNIS COURTS (#)
  o JACUZZI (#)
  o SAUNA (#)
  ● BIKEPATHS
  o FIELD GAMES
  ● OTHER

  o MAINTENANCE OF EXTERIOR
  o INSURANCE
  o WATER
  o MAINT. COMMON SPACE
  o OTHER:

BUYER PROFILE:
Average Age: 28-34
# of Children   1.5%
Average Income:

Prev. Residence:
Both Spouses Work:
Occupation Category:

FINANCING OFFERED:
  o FHA
  o VA

  ● CONVENTIONAL
  o OTHER

SALES PROFILE AND HISTORY:
Date Opened:
Weekly Sales Rate:

Sold to Date:
Total Unsold:

MATERIALS TO OBTAIN:
  ● Sales Brochure
  o Price List
  o Floor Plans
  o Deed Restrictions
  ● Covenants

  o Photographs
  o Site Plan
  o Approved Development Plan
  o HOA Documents

INTERVIEWER: David R. Jensen

Development Concept
Planning Form

DEVELOPMENT: Woodbridge Gables
LOCATION: Irvine, CA

DEVELOPER: Irvine Pacific

DATE: 4/80

DATE OPENED: 1978
DATE FINISHED:

1,238 total acres
HOUSING CONCEPT: SF Zero Lot Line cluster
DENSITY: 5.5
% OPEN SPACE: 15% (191 acres)
ORGANIZATION OF OPEN SPACE: lakes, trails, bike
    paths, private parks, community parks

ZONING: medium density R-1
SETBACKS: front 5' min.
PROJECT SIZE: 160 units
LOT SIZES:5000 sq. ft.

PLAN #/NAME	(1) W7/9A	(2) W7/9B	(3) W7/9C	(4) W7/9D	(5) W7/9E
PRICE:	87,500	90,000	95,000	100,000	105,000
SQUARE FEET:	1750	1900	2100	2250	2400
# OF LEVELS	1	1	2	2	2
BEDROOMS	3	3+	3+	4	5
BATHS	2	2	2½	3	3
GARAGE (detached)	2	2	2	2	2
PLAN MIX	16%(30)	22%(40)	16%(30)	22%(40)	24%(45)
# SOLD	"	"	"	"	"

PHYSICAL CHARACTER:

EXTERIOR:
  ROOF: shake
  SIDING: wood and stucco
  DRIVEWAY: Concrete
  FENCING: wood
  LANDSCAPING: no
  SPRINKLERS:
  ARCH. TYPE: Calif. Contemporary
  COLORS: traditional

PLANNING FEATURES:
  PARKING: gar./drive./street
  STREET LAYOUT:loops and culs
  STREET WIDTHS:46 row/36 pav.
  SPECIAL FEATURES:
  INNOVATIONS:
  ENTRY:
  COMMON AREAS:
  IMAGE:
  BUILDING SEPARATIONS:
  ENERGY FEATURES:

Woodbridge Gables
HOMEOWNERS ASSOCIATION:

MONTHLY ASSESSMENT: $25.00
RECREATION FEE:

INCLUDES:
  o CLUBHOUSE/REC. ROOM
  o SWIMMING POOL (#)
  o TENNIS COURTS (#)
  o JACUZZI (#)
  o SAUNA (#)
  ● BIKEPATHS (Community)
  o FIELD GAMES
  ● OTHER   Open Space (Community)

  o MAINTENANCE OF EXTERIOR
  o INSURANCE
  o WATER
  o MAINT. COMMON SPACE
  o OTHER:

BUYER PROFILE:
Average Age: 25-40
# of Children 1.5 av. (0-15 years)
Average Income: $35,000-50,000

Prev. Residence: SF det
Both Spouses Work: Yes
Occupation Category: Young management

FINANCING OFFERED:
  o FHA
  o VA

  ● CONVENTIONAL
  o OTHER

SALES PROFILE AND HISTORY:
Date Opened: 1978
Weekly Sales Rate:

Sold to Date: 100%
Total Unsold:

MATERIALS TO OBTAIN:
  ● Sales Brochure
  o Price List
  o Floor Plans
  o Deed Restrictions
  ● Covenants

  o Photographs
  ● Site Plan
  ● Approved Development Plan
  o HOA Documents

INTERVIEWER: David R. Jensen

Development Concept
Planning Form

DEVELOPMENT: Palacio del Mar   DATE: 4/80
LOCATION: San Clemente, CA
                                      DATE OPENED: 9/79
DEVELOPER: Stein, Brief Group   DATE FINISHED:
            Irvine, CA

HOUSING CONCEPT: Zero Lot Line   ZONING: R-1, B-1, PRD
DENSITY: 2.23/acre   SETBACKS: vary (5')
% OPEN SPACE: 54% (21 acres - slope) PROJECT SIZE: 68 units
ORGANIZATION OF OPEN SPACE: HOA/slopes LOT SIZES: 50 x 80

PLAN #/NAME	(1)	(2)	(3)	(4)
PRICE:	275,000	319,000	334,000	
SQUARE FEET:	2,000	2,650	2,750	
# OF LEVELS	1	3	3	
BEDROOMS	2+1	2+2	3+ loft	
BATHS	2	2	2 ½	
GARAGE	2	2	3	
PLAN MIX	11	13	12	
# SOLD	7	9	9	

PHYSICAL CHARACTER:

EXTERIOR: PLANNING FEATURES:
  ROOF: tile   PARKING:
  SIDING: STREET LAYOUT:
  DRIVEWAY: concrete   STREET WIDTHS:
  FENCING: block   SPECIAL FEATURES:
  LANDSCAPING: front   INNOVATIONS:
  SPRINKLERS: front   ENTRY:
  ARCH. TYPE: COMMON AREAS:
  COLORS: IMAGE:
                                        BUILDING SEPARATIONS:
                                        ENERGY FEATURES:

Palacio del Mar
HOMEOWNERS ASSOCIATION: MONTHLY ASSESSMENT:
                                       RECREATION FEE:

INCLUDES:
  o CLUBHOUSE/REC. ROOM   o MAINTENANCE OF EXTERIOR
  o SWIMMING POOL (#)   o INSURANCE
  o TENNIS COURTS (#)   o WATER
  o JACUZZI (#)   o MAINT. COMMON SPACE
  o SAUNA (#)   o OTHER:
  o BIKEPATHS
  o FIELD GAMES
  o OTHER

BUYER PROFILE:
Average Age: Prev. Residence:
# of Children   Both Spouses Work:
Average Income: Occupation Category:

FINANCING OFFERED:
  o FHA   ● CONVENTIONAL
  o VA   o OTHER

SALES PROFILE AND HISTORY:
Date Opened: 9/79   # Sold to Date: 25
Weekly Sales Rate: .89   Total Unsold: 11

MATERIALS TO OBTAIN:
  o Sales Brochure   o Photographs
  o Price List   o Site Plan
  o Floor Plans   o Approved Development Plan
  o Deed Restrictions   o HOA Documents
  o Covenants
                                       INTERVIEWER: David R. Jensen

DEVELOPMENT: Isle of Pines
LOCATION: Sea Pines Plantation
         Hilton Head, S.C.
DEVELOPER: Austin Construction & Development
              Company

DATE: 8/30/80

DATE OPENED: 12/80
DATE FINISHED:

HOUSING CONCEPT: Custom Zero Lot Line Patio
DENSITY: 4.5 du/ac   Homes
% OPEN SPACE: ½ acre
ORGANIZATION OF OPEN SPACE: Part of master Sea
      Pines Plantation Assn.

ZONING: Res with C and R
SETBACKS: 10' off asphalt
PROJECT SIZE: 7.21 ac/30 du
LOT SIZES: 60 x 100

PLAN #/NAME	(1)	(2)	(3)	(4)
	61	28	30	
PRICE:	$139,500	$160,000	$215,000	
SQUARE FEET:	1,730	2,400	2,400	
# OF LEVELS	1	1	1	
BEDROOMS	2	3	3	
BATHS	2	3	3	
GARAGE	1½-car	2-car	2-car	

Lots: $45,000-50,000

PLAN MIX
SOLD

PHYSICAL CHARACTER:

EXTERIOR:
  ROOF: asphalt shingles
  SIDING: cypress or cedar board
  DRIVEWAY: concrete
  FENCING: vertical cypress or cedar
  LANDSCAPING: yes, $2,500
  SPRINKLERS: yes
  ARCH. TYPE: contemporary
  COLORS: earth tones

PLANNING FEATURES:
  PARKING: 3-4 spaces
  STREET LAYOUT: cul de sac
  STREET WIDTHS: 50' ROW/20' pave
  SPECIAL FEATURES: Central openspace
  INNOVATIONS: View oriented to G.C.
                  and lagoons
  ENTRY:
  COMMON AREAS: ½ acre
  IMAGE: quality
  BUILDING SEPARATIONS: 10'
  ENERGY FEATURES: none

Isle Of Pines
HOMEOWNERS ASSOCIATION: No
    Master Sea Pine Plantation Property
      Owner Assn.

INCLUDES:
  o CLUBHOUSE/REC. ROOM
  o SWIMMING POOL (#)
  o TENNIS COURTS (#)
  o JACUZZI (#)
  o SAUNA (#)
  ● BIKEPATHS
  o FIELD GAMES
  ● OTHER Fishing lagoons
            Forest preserve

Annual
MONTHLY ASSESSMENT: $200.00
RECREATION FEE: Private clubs

  o MAINTENANCE OF EXTERIOR
  o INSURANCE
  o WATER
  ● MAINT. COMMON SPACE
  ● OTHER: Roads
            Security

BUYER PROFILE:
Average Age: Retirees and vacation oriented
# of Children
Average Income:

Prev. Residence: NE US
Both Spouses Work:
Occupation Category: upper
                   management

FINANCING OFFERED:
  o FHA
  o VA

  ● CONVENTIONAL 50%
  ● OTHER 50% cash

SALES PROFILE AND HISTORY:
Date Opened: 12/80
Weekly Sales Rate:

Sold to Date: 25
Total Unsold: 8

MATERIALS TO OBTAIN:
  o Sales Brochure
  o Price List
  ● Floor Plans
  o Deed Restrictions
  ● Covenants

  ● Photographs
  ● Site Plan
  o Approved Development Plan
  o HOA Documents

INTERVIEWER: David R. Jensen

Development Concept
Planning Form

DEVELOPMENT: Otter Road Subdivision
LOCATION: Sea Pines Plantation
         Hilton Head, S.C.
DEVELOPER: Austin Construction & Development
              Company

DATE: 8/30/80

DATE OPENED: 1972
DATE FINISHED:

HOUSING CONCEPT: Zero Lot Line Patio Homes
DENSITY: 4.3 du/ac
% OPEN SPACE: 6.01 acres 18%
ORGANIZATION OF OPEN SPACE:

ZONING: Res with C and R
SETBACKS: F 20; S 3+7; R 15
PROJECT SIZE: 33 ac/142du
LOT SIZES: 60 x 100

PLAN #/NAME	(1) Seabrook	(2) Altamoa	(3) Alpine	(4)
PRICE:	$90,000	$77,000	$85,000	
SQUARE FEET:	1,582	1,248	1,700	
# OF LEVELS	1	1	2	
BEDROOMS	3	3	2	
BATHS	2	2	2	
GARAGE	2	1½	1	

PLAN MIX

SOLD   Custom

PHYSICAL CHARACTER:

EXTERIOR:
  ROOF: asphalt shingles
  SIDING: cedar
  DRIVEWAY: asphalt
  FENCING: vertical cedar
  LANDSCAPING: no
  SPRINKLERS: no
  ARCH. TYPE: contemporary
  COLORS: earth tones

PLANNING FEATURES:
  PARKING: 1½ gar; 2 driveway
  STREET LAYOUT: loop and culs
  STREET WIDTHS: 50' Row; 20' pave
  SPECIAL FEATURES: golf edge, open-
                space backyard
  INNOVATIONS: Headless culs
  ENTRY:
  COMMON AREAS:
  IMAGE:
  BUILDING SEPARATIONS: 10'
  ENERGY FEATURES:

Otter Road Subdivision

HOMEOWNERS ASSOCIATION:

  Sea Pines Plantation
  Owners Assn.
INCLUDES:
  o CLUBHOUSE/REC. ROOM
  o SWIMMING POOL (#)
  o TENNIS COURTS (#)
  o JACUZZI (#)
  o SAUNA (#)
  o BIKEPATHS
  o FIELD GAMES
  o OTHER

X̶M̶O̶N̶X̶H̶L̶X̶X̶ ASSESSMENT: $200/yr.
RECREATION FEE:

  o MAINTENANCE OF EXTERIOR
  o INSURANCE
  o WATER
  o MAINT. COMMON SPACE
  o OTHER:

BUYER PROFILE:
Average Age: Retirees and younger
# of Children   some
Average Income:

Prev. Residence: local and NE US
Both Spouses Work:
Occupation Category: Retired

FINANCING OFFERED:
  o FHA
  o VA

  ● CONVENTIONAL 50%
  ● OTHER   50% cash

SALES PROFILE AND HISTORY:
Date Opened: 1972
Weekly Sales Rate:

Sold to Date: 60%
Total Unsold: 40%

MATERIALS TO OBTAIN:
  o Sales Brochure
  o Price List
  ● Floor Plans
  o Deed Restrictions
  ● Covenants

  ● Photographs
  ● Site Plan
  o Approved Development Plan
  o HOA Documents

INTERVIEWER: David R. Jensen

Development Concept
Planning Form

HOH Associates, Inc.

DEVELOPMENT: 5000 sq. ft.   DATE:
LOCATION: Oahu, Hawaii
                                                 DATE OPENED: 7/78
DEVELOPER: Gentry - Waipio J.V.   DATE FINISHED:

HOUSING CONCEPT: Zero Lot Line   ZONING:
DENSITY: 6.5 du/ac   SETBACKS: 10' (18-20 to gar)
% OPEN SPACE: 20 out of 500 acres (4%)   PROJECT SIZE: 12-14 ac
ORGANIZATION OF OPEN SPACE: Trees, walks   LOT SIZES: 5000 sq. ft.
     (100 du planned - part of larger project)

---

	(1)	(2)	(3)	(4)
PLAN #/NAME	4 models			
PRICE:	140,000-180,000			
SQUARE FEET:	1657-2379			
# OF LEVELS	1 and 2			
BEDROOMS	3 and 4			
BATHS	2 and 2½			
GARAGE	2-car			
PLAN MIX	even			
# SOLD	250 total			

PHYSICAL CHARACTER:

EXTERIOR: PLANNING FEATURES:
  ROOF: Cedar shake   PARKING: 2 garage/2 driveway
  SIDING: Wood frame   STREET LAYOUT: curve and culs
  DRIVEWAY: Concrete   STREET WIDTHS: 40 and 28
  FENCING: 6' redwood   SPECIAL FEATURES:
  LANDSCAPING: No   INNOVATIONS:
  SPRINKLERS: ENTRY:
  ARCH. TYPE: COMMON AREAS:
  COLORS: Earth   IMAGE:
                                           BUILDING SEPARATIONS:
                                           ENERGY FEATURES:

5000 sq. ft. - Oahu, Hawaii
HOMEOWNERS ASSOCIATION: MONTHLY ASSESSMENT: $50/yr.
                                          RECREATION FEE:

INCLUDES:
  o CLUBHOUSE/REC. ROOM   o MAINTENANCE OF EXTERIOR
  o SWIMMING POOL (#)   o INSURANCE
  o TENNIS COURTS (#)   o WATER
  o JACUZZI (#)   o MAINT. COMMON SPACE
  o SAUNA (#)   o OTHER:
  ● BIKEPATHS
  o FIELD GAMES
  o OTHER

BUYER PROFILE:
Average Age: 35-40   Prev. Residence: within 5 miles
# of Children 2   Both Spouses Work: Yes
Average Income: $40,000   Occupation Category: All

FINANCING OFFERED:
  o FHA   ● CONVENTIONAL
  o VA   o OTHER

SALES PROFILE AND HISTORY:
Date Opened: 1978   # Sold to Date: 250
Weekly Sales Rate: Total Unsold:

MATERIALS TO OBTAIN:
  ● Sales Brochure   o Photographs
  o Price List   ● Site Plan
  o Floor Plans   o Approved Development Plan
  o Deed Restrictions   o HOA Documents
  ● Covenants

                    INTERVIEWER: David R. Jensen

HOH Associates, Inc.

DEVELOPMENT: Kingston Dunes
LOCATION: Shipyard Plantation
          Hilton Head, S.C.
DEVELOPER:
          The Hilton Head Company

DATE: 10/29/80

DATE OPENED: 1977
DATE FINISHED:

                  Sale of lots for custom
HOUSING CONCEPT: Zero Lot Line patio homes
DENSITY: 4 du/ac
% OPEN SPACE: 3 acres
ORGANIZATION OF OPEN SPACE:

ZONING: Res with C and R
SETBACKS: 35'F; 50'R; 1+3S
PROJECT SIZE: 49 du
LOT SIZES: 50 x 160

	(1)	(2)	(3)	(4)
PLAN #/NAME				
PRICE:	$113,000 - $186,000			
SQUARE FEET:	1,200 - 2,800			
# OF LEVELS				
BEDROOMS	Custom Homes			
BATHS	Lots: $22,000 - 23,000			
GARAGE				
PLAN MIX				
# SOLD				

PHYSICAL CHARACTER:

EXTERIOR:
  ROOF:
  SIDING: cypress and stucco
  DRIVEWAY:
  FENCING:
  LANDSCAPING:
  SPRINKLERS:
  ARCH. TYPE:
  COLORS:

PLANNING FEATURES:
  PARKING:
  STREET LAYOUT:
  STREET WIDTHS:
  SPECIAL FEATURES:
  INNOVATIONS:
  ENTRY:
  COMMON AREAS:
  IMAGE:
  BUILDING SEPARATIONS:
  ENERGY FEATURES:

Kingston Dunes
HOMEOWNERS ASSOCIATION:

MONTHLY ASSESSMENT: $181.00
RECREATION FEE:

Overall Property Owners Assn.

INCLUDES:
  o CLUBHOUSE/REC. ROOM
  o SWIMMING POOL (#)
  o TENNIS COURTS (#)
  o JACUZZI (#)
  o SAUNA (#)
  o BIKEPATHS
  o FIELD GAMES
  o OTHER

  o MAINTENANCE OF EXTERIOR
  o INSURANCE
  o WATER
  o MAINT. COMMON SPACE
  ● OTHER:
           Roads and beaches
           Security

BUYER PROFILE:
Average Age:
# of Children
Average Income:

Prev. Residence:
Both Spouses Work:
Occupation Category:

FINANCING OFFERED:
  o FHA
  o VA

  o CONVENTIONAL
  o OTHER

SALES PROFILE AND HISTORY:
Date Opened: 1977
Weekly Sales Rate:

Sold to Date:
Total Unsold: None

MATERIALS TO OBTAIN:
  o Sales Brochure
  o Price List
  o Floor Plans
  o Deed Restrictions
  o Covenants

  o Photographs
  o Site Plan
  o Approved Development Plan
  o HOA Documents

INTERVIEWER: David R. Jensen

Development Concept
Planning Form

HOH Associates, Inc.

DEVELOPMENT: Misty Cove
LOCATION: Shipyard Plantation
         Hilton Head, S.C.
DEVELOPER: Twin Oaks Development

DATE: 10/29/80

DATE OPENED: 1978
DATE FINISHED:

HOUSING CONCEPT: Zero Lot Line Patio Homes
DENSITY:
% OPEN SPACE: Buffer Areas
ORGANIZATION OF OPEN SPACE:

ZONING: Res with C and R
SETBACKS: 35R; 1+3S; 35R
PROJECT SIZE: 22 du
LOT SIZES: 50 x 150

PLAN #/NAME	(1)	(2)	(3)	(4)
PRICE:	$108,000	$112,000	$118,000	
SQUARE FEET:	1,580	1,600	1,500-1,800	
# OF LEVELS	1	1	1	
BEDROOMS	2	2	3	
BATHS	2	2	2	
GARAGE	1½-car	1½-car	1½-car	

PLAN MIX
SOLD

PHYSICAL CHARACTER:

EXTERIOR:

ROOF: asphalt shingle
SIDING: cypress siding with stucco
DRIVEWAY: asphalt
FENCING: stucco
LANDSCAPING: $1,200/du
SPRINKLERS: yes
ARCH. TYPE: modern
COLORS: earth tones

PLANNING FEATURES:

PARKING: 1½/unit required
STREET LAYOUT: culs
STREET WIDTHS: 20' pavements
SPECIAL FEATURES: golf frontage
INNOVATIONS:
ENTRY:
COMMON AREAS: yes
IMAGE: permanent residents
BUILDING SEPARATIONS: 6'
ENERGY FEATURES:

Misty Cove
HOMEOWNERS ASSOCIATION: yes

MONTHLY ASSESSMENT: $100/yr.
RECREATION FEE:

INCLUDES:

o CLUBHOUSE/REC. ROOM
o SWIMMING POOL (#)
o TENNIS COURTS (#)
o JACUZZI (#)
o SAUNA (#)
o BIKEPATHS
o FIELD GAMES
o OTHER

o MAINTENANCE OF EXTERIOR
o INSURANCE
o WATER
● MAINT. COMMON SPACE
● OTHER
        Roads
        Beaches
        Security

BUYER PROFILE:

Average Age: 55
# of Children minimum
Average Income: $50,000 +

Prev. Residence: out of state
Both Spouses Work: no
Occupation Category: executive with
                    some retired

FINANCING OFFERED:

o FHA
o VA

● CONVENTIONAL
● OTHER cash

SALES PROFILE AND HISTORY:
Date Opened: late 1978
Weekly Sales Rate:

Sold to Date:
Total Unsold: 4

MATERIALS TO OBTAIN:

o Sales Brochure
o Price List
o Floor Plans
o Deed Restrictions
o Covenants

o Photographs
o Site Plan
o Approved Development Plan
o HOA Documents

INTERVIEWER: David R. Jensen

**Development Concept
Planning Form**

DEVELOPMENT: The Crossings
LOCATION: Dade County, Florida

DEVELOPER: Arvida Corporation

DATE: 8/80

DATE OPENED: 11/76
DATE FINISHED: 6/80

HOUSING CONCEPT: Zero Lot Line Cluster
DENSITY: 4.8 du/ac
% OPEN SPACE: 40% code required
ORGANIZATION OF OPEN SPACE:

ZONING: RU - 1C
SETBACKS:
PROJECT SIZE: 105 ac/501 du
LOT SIZES: 55 x 80

PLAN #/NAME	(1) Galloway	(2) York	(3) Kent	(4) Stratford	(5) Nottingham
PRICE:	$71,000	$84,000	$84,500	$91,000	$96,500
SQUARE FEET:	1,080	1,320	1,315	1,600	1,680
# OF LEVELS	1	1	1	1	2
BEDROOMS	2	3	3	3	-
BATHS	1½	2	2	2	-
GARAGE	1-car	1-car	1-car	2-car	2-car
PLAN MIX	28%	34%	15%	14%	10%
# SOLD	138	168	73	71	50

PHYSICAL CHARACTER:

EXTERIOR:
  ROOF: asphalt shingle
  SIDING: stucco and rough sawn cedar
  DRIVEWAY: asphalt
  FENCING: pressure treated pine
  LANDSCAPING: yes
  SPRINKLERS:
  ARCH. TYPE: Calif. contemp.
  COLORS: earth tones

PLANNING FEATURES:
  PARKING: 3-4 spaces
  STREET LAYOUT: culs and loops
  STREET WIDTHS: 20' pavement
  SPECIAL FEATURES: no sidewalks
  INNOVATIONS:
  ENTRY:
  COMMON AREAS: yes
  IMAGE: professional
  BUILDING SEPARATIONS: 10'
  ENERGY FEATURES:

The Crossings
HOMEOWNERS ASSOCIATION: yes

MONTHLY ASSESSMENT: $31 and $22.00
RECREATION FEE:

INCLUDES:
  ● CLUBHOUSE/REC. ROOM Cabana
  ● SWIMMING POOL (#)
  ● TENNIS COURTS (#)
  ● JACUZZI (#)
  o SAUNA (#)
  ● BIKEPATHS
  ● FIELD GAMES
  ● OTHER Tot Lots

  o MAINTENANCE OF EXTERIOR
  o INSURANCE
  o WATER
  ● MAINT. COMMON SPACE
  o OTHER:

BUYER PROFILE:
Average Age: 25-45
# of Children
Average Income: $35,000

Prev. Residence: Miami area
Both Spouses Work: more than 50%
Occupation Category: professional, self employed

FINANCING OFFERED:
  o FHA
  o VA

  ● CONVENTIONAL
  o OTHER

SALES PROFILE AND HISTORY:
Date Opened: 11/76
Weekly Sales Rate:

Sold to Date: 100%
Total Unsold: 0

MATERIALS TO OBTAIN:
  o Sales Brochure
  o Price List
  o Floor Plans
  o Deed Restrictions
  o Covenants

  o Photographs
  o Site Plan
  o Approved Development Plan
  o HOA Documents

INTERVIEWER: David R. Jensen

Development Concept
Planning Form

DEVELOPMENT: "The Greens" of Emerald Hills
LOCATION: Hollywood, Florida

DEVELOPER: Hollywood, Inc

DATE: 8/28/80

DATE OPENED: 5/78
DATE FINISHED: 12/79

HOUSING CONCEPT: Patio Home with Zero Lot Line
DENSITY: 5 du/ac
% OPEN SPACE: ½ acre
ORGANIZATION OF OPEN SPACE:

ZONING: M.F.; PUD
SETBACKS: none
PROJECT SIZE: 150 d.u.
LOT SIZES: 55' - 60' x 80'

PLAN #/NAME	(1) A	(2) B	(3) C	(4) D
PRICE: *	$79,900	$85,900	$89,900	86,900
SQUARE FEET:	1,946	2,156	2,295	2,137
# OF LEVELS	1	1	2	1
BEDROOMS	3	3	4	3
BATHS	2½	2½	3	2½
GARAGE	2-car	2-car	2-car	2-car
PLAN MIX	43%	37%	40%	30%
# SOLD				

* March, 1978; plus premium for location

PHYSICAL CHARACTER:

EXTERIOR:
  ROOF: asphalt shingles
  SIDING: stucco
  DRIVEWAY: asphalt
  FENCING: wood vertical cedar
  LANDSCAPING: yes
  SPRINKLERS: yes
  ARCH. TYPE:
  COLORS: earth tones

PLANNING FEATURES:
  PARKING: 4 spaces
  STREET LAYOUT: loop with culs
  STREET WIDTHS: 22'
  SPECIAL FEATURES: golf course
  INNOVATIONS: planned islands in culs and loops
  ENTRY:
  COMMON AREAS:
  IMAGE: modern
  BUILDING SEPARATIONS: 7½'
  ENERGY FEATURES: no

Units are attached by trellises to meet zoning and
avoid setbacks between buildings.

"The Greens" of Emerald Hills
HOMEOWNERS ASSOCIATION: yes

MONTHLY ASSESSMENT: $69.00
RECREATION FEE: No

INCLUDES:
  o CLUBHOUSE/REC. ROOM
  ● SWIMMING POOL (#) with each home
  o TENNIS COURTS (#)
  o JACUZZI (#)
  o SAUNA (#)
  ● BIKEPATHS along street
  o FIELD GAMES
  o OTHER

  o MAINTENANCE OF EXTERIOR
  o INSURANCE
  o WATER
  ● MAINT. COMMON SPACE
  ● OTHER:
      Garbage pickup
      Front yard maint.

  This project is a part of a larger one that provides recreation and
  marketing plan.

BUYER PROFILE:
Average Age: 55
# of Children very few
Average Income: high

                              60% community
Prev. Residence: 40% out of town
Both Spouses Work:
Occupation Category: professional

FINANCING OFFERED:
  o FHA
  o VA

  ● CONVENTIONAL
  ● OTHER cash

SALES PROFILE AND HISTORY:
Date Opened: 5/78
Weekly Sales Rate: 8-10

Sold to Date: 150
Total Unsold: none

MATERIALS TO OBTAIN:
  ● Sales Brochure
  ● Price List
  ● Floor Plans
  o Deed Restrictions
  o Covenants

  ● Condominum documents
  ● Photographs
  ● Site Plan
  o Approved Development Plan
  o HOA Documents

INTERVIEWER: David R. Jensen

Development Concept
Planning Form

DEVELOPMENT: "The Woods" of Emerald Hills   DATE: 8/28/80
LOCATION: Hollywood, Florida

DATE OPENED: 1977
DEVELOPER: Hollywood, Inc.   DATE FINISHED: 1978

HOUSING CONCEPT: Patio Home Zero Lot Line   ZONING: PUD for MF
DENSITY: 5du/ac   Attached trellises   SETBACKS: none
% OPEN SPACE: no   PROJECT SIZE: 60du/12ac
ORGANIZATION OF OPEN SPACE: LOT SIZES: 55-60 x 85

PLAN #/NAME	(1) A	(2) B	(3) C	(4) D
PRICE: (1977)	$69,990	$74,990	$79,990	$75,990
SQUARE FEET:				
# OF LEVELS	1	1	2	1
BEDROOMS	3	3	4	3
BATHS	2½	2½	3	2½
GARAGE	2	2	2	2
PLAN MIX	20%	30%	25%	25%
# SOLD	12	18	15	15

(sold out in 30 days)

PHYSICAL CHARACTER:

EXTERIOR:
   ROOF: asphalt shingles
   SIDING: stucco
   DRIVEWAY: asphalt
   FENCING: vertical wood cedar
   LANDSCAPING: yes
   SPRINKLERS: yes
   ARCH. TYPE:
   COLORS: earth tones

PLANNING FEATURES:
   PARKING: 2 gar./2 drive.
   STREET LAYOUT: loop with culs
   STREET WIDTHS: 22'
   SPECIAL FEATURES: planted islands in culs
   INNOVATIONS: special design of street lighting and signs
   ENTRY:
   COMMON AREAS:
   IMAGE:
   BUILDING SEPARATIONS: 7½'
   ENERGY FEATURES:

This project is part of a larger one that provides overall recreation and marketing plan.

"The Woods" of Emerald Hills
HOMEOWNERS ASSOCIATION: Yes   MONTHLY ASSESSMENT: $49.00
RECREATION FEE:

INCLUDES:
   o CLUBHOUSE/REC. ROOM
   ● SWIMMING POOL (#) provided with each home
   o TENNIS COURTS (#)
   o JACUZZI (#)
   o SAUNA (#)
   o BIKEPATHS
   o FIELD GAMES
   o OTHER

   o MAINTENANCE OF EXTERIOR
   o INSURANCE
   o WATER
   ● MAINT. COMMON SPACE
   ● OTHER:
      Street lights and signs
      Streets
      Front yards

BUYER PROFILE:
Average Age: 55
# of Children few
Average Income: high

Prev. Residence: 60% community
Both Spouses Work: 40% out of town
Occupation Category: Professional

FINANCING OFFERED:
   o FHA
   o VA

   ● CONVENTIONAL
   ● OTHER cash

SALES PROFILE AND HISTORY:
Date Opened: May 1977   # Sold to Date:
Weekly Sales Rate: 14   Total Unsold:

MATERIALS TO OBTAIN:
   o Sales Brochure
   o Price List
   o Floor Plans
   o Deed Restrictions
   o Covenants

   o Photographs
   o Site Plan
   o Approved Development Plan
   o HOA Documents

INTERVIEWER: David R. Jensen

Development Concept
Planning Form

DEVELOPMENT: Lexington Green
LOCATION: Virginia Beach, Virginia

DATE: November 3, 1980

DEVELOPER: Peterson Associates
(John Peterson)

DATE OPENED: Not opened yet
DATE FINISHED: ------

HOUSING CONCEPT: Zero Lot Line Det.
DENSITY: 5.5 DU/AC
% OPEN SPACE: Corridor walkway behind units
ORGANIZATION OF OPEN SPACE:

ZONING: P.U.D.
SETBACKS: Approx. 25'
PROJECT SIZE: 20-30 lots
LOT SIZES: 37' x 100'

PLAN #/NAME	(1) A	(2) B	(3) C	(4) D
PRICE:	$46,000	$47,500	$53,500	$51,500
SQUARE FEET:				
# OF LEVELS	1	1	2	1
BEDROOMS	2	2	3	3
BATHS	1	2	2	2
GARAGE	No	No	No	No
PLAN MIX	As sold			
# SOLD	None			

PHYSICAL CHARACTER:

EXTERIOR:
ROOF: Brown Asphalt 5:12
SIDING: Vinyl siding (Horz)
DRIVEWAY: 2 Concrete Pad
FENCING: Of Front Court
LANDSCAPING: Good in Models ($1500/unit) Entry Level Price Prohibits
SPRINKLERS: No
ARCH. TYPE: Contemporary
COLORS: Greys Field/White trim

PLANNING FEATURES:
PARKING: 2 car pad in front
STREET LAYOUT: Cul de Sac
STREET WIDTHS: 30'
SPECIAL FEATURES: Great Room
INNOVATIONS: Outstorage - intregal part of
ENTRY: entry
COMMON AREAS: None
IMAGE: Clean - interesting
BUILDING SEPARATIONS: 10' Min
ENERGY FEATURES: Heat pump
R-26 ceiling
insul. (V.H.
insul. front Dr.

Lexington Green

HOMEOWNERS ASSOCIATION: Same as Green Run

MONTHLY ASSESSMENT:
RECREATION FEE:

INCLUDES:
o CLUBHOUSE/REC. ROOM
o SWIMMING POOL (#)
o TENNIS COURTS (#)
o JACUZZI (#)
o SAUNA (#)
o BIKEPATHS
o FIELD GAMES
o OTHER

o MAINTENANCE OF EXTERIOR
o INSURANCE
o WATER
o MAINT. COMMON SPACE
o OTHER:
Marketing: Has small pool in side
yard of one model

BUYER PROFILE: N.A.
Average Age:
# of Children
Average Income:

Prev. Residence:
Both Spouses Work:
Occupation Category:

FINANCING OFFERED:
● FHA
● VA

● CONVENTIONAL
o OTHER

SALES PROFILE AND HISTORY:
Date Opened: Not
Weekly Sales Rate:

Sold to Date:
Total Unsold:

MATERIALS TO OBTAIN:
● Sales Brochure
● Price List
o Floor Plans
o Deed Restrictions   Same as Green Run
o Covenants

● Photographs
o Site Plan
o Approved Development Plan
o HOA Documents

INTERVIEWER: Jay Parker

Development Concept
Planning Form

Bob Long, Whitman, Requardt
DATE: Oct. 29, 1980

DEVELOPMENT: Monterey Court
LOCATION: Columbia, Md.

DATE OPENED: Spring 70) 1st section
DATE FINISHED: Spring 71) 57

DEVELOPER: Howard Homes
  Land Design Research, Fred Jarvis 620-3650

UNITS: 57 units first phase
ZONING: PUD (new town)
SETBACKS: Bldg. 30' garages forward
PROJECT SIZE: 10 ac.   (exception)
LOT SIZES: 60 x 200

HOUSING CONCEPT: S.F.D. zero - shared garages
DENSITY: 5.5 du/ac
% OPEN SPACE:
ORGANIZATION OF OPEN SPACE:

	(1)	(2)	(3)	(4)
PLAN #/NAME				
PRICE:	$30,000		$33,000	
SQUARE FEET:				
# OF LEVELS				
BEDROOMS	3	3	4	
BATHS	1 3/4	1 3/4	2	
GARAGE	1	1	1	
PLAN MIX				
# SOLD				

PHYSICAL CHARACTER:

EXTERIOR:

ROOF: Asphalt 5:12
SIDING: stained plywood, exposed painted block
DRIVEWAY: concrete
FENCING: Solid board & batt to match house
LANDSCAPING: Extensive w/ street trees, primarily evergreen
SPRINKLERS: no
ARCH. TYPE: California Contemporary
COLORS: Block painted light tan
        All other colors very dark brown

PLANNING FEATURES:
PARKING: some shared garages; 1 gar. space, 1 driveway space
STREET LAYOUT: Short culs, cul heads linked w/ paths
STREET WIDTHS: vertical curb 30'
SPECIAL FEATURES:
INNOVATIONS: end of cul siting
ENTRY: open to street
COMMON AREAS: limited
IMAGE: Rustic - a little rough; very nice
BUILDING SEPARATIONS: 15"±
ENERGY FEATURES:

Monterey Court
HOMEOWNERS ASSOCIATION:

MONTHLY ASSESSMENT: fee simple
RECREATION FEE: only Columbia Assoc.

INCLUDES:

o CLUBHOUSE/REC. ROOM
o SWIMMING POOL (#)
o TENNIS COURTS (#)
o JACUZZI (#)
o SAUNA (#)
o BIKEPATHS
o FIELD GAMES
o OTHER

o MAINTENANCE OF EXTERIOR
o INSURANCE
o WATER
o MAINT. COMMON SPACE
o OTHER:
    4' subservient maintenance easement granting other party easement

BUYER PROFILE:
Average Age: 28-30
# of Children 1-2
Average Income: $25 - 30,000

Prev. Residence: Local
Both Spouses Work: Yes
Occupation Category: sophisticated-management levels

FINANCING OFFERED:
● FHA
● VA

● CONVENTIONAL
o OTHER

SALES PROFILE AND HISTORY:
Date Opened: Spring '70
Weekly Sales Rate: 1 - 2

Sold to Date: 117 (1st + 2nd phase)
Total Unsold: 0

MATERIALS TO OBTAIN:
o Sales Brochure
o Price List
o Floor Plans
o Deed Restrictions
o Covenants

o Photographs
o Site Plan
o Approved Development Plan
o HOA Documents

INTERVIEWER: Jay Parker

142

Development Concept
Planning Form

Courts of Whetstone

DEVELOPMENT: Courts of Whetstone
LOCATION: Montgomery Village, MD

DATE: October 29, 1980

DEVELOPER: Kettler Brothers
            RTKL Architects

DATE OPENED: March, 1968
DATE FINISHED: January, 1971

HOUSING CONCEPT: S.F.D. Zeros
DENSITY: 4.3 du/ac
% OPEN SPACE: 32.7 %
ORGANIZATION OF OPEN SPACE: Finger O.S. backs of
                           units

ZONING: PUD
SETBACKS: None req. - 0 setback
PROJECT SIZE: 105 du/24.3 ac.
LOT SIZES: 4,300 avg.

PLAN #/NAME	(1) Wellington	(2) Montreal	(3) Windsor	(4)
PRICE:	49,950	52,500	59,950	

r., '70 SQUARE FEET:

# OF LEVELS	3	3	3	
BEDROOMS	4	4+	5+	
BATHS	2½	2½	2, 2½	
GARAGE	2 car	2 car	2 car	

PLAN MIX

SOLD

PHYSICAL CHARACTER:

EXTERIOR:

ROOF: Asphalt   5:12 Pitch (good)
SIDING: Texture 111 and brick
DRIVEWAY: Asphalt
FENCING: Entire lot brick fence
LANDSCAPING: Elaborate
SPRINKLERS: no
ARCH. TYPE: Calif. contemporary
COLORS: Light brick and earth tones

PLANNING FEATURES:
PARKING: 2 garage spaces and "random"
         court park.
STREET LAYOUT:
STREET WIDTHS: 30' min. bet. bldg.,
              20' rdwy. private
SPECIAL FEATURES: Library
INNOVATIONS: "random" parking
ENTRY: Courtyard
COMMON AREAS: pathways and lands.
IMAGE: very attractive, sophisticated
BUILDING SEPARATIONS: 5' min.
ENERGY FEATURES:

HOMEOWNERS ASSOCIATION: Homes "Corp."
Includes some S.F. conventional
Can also belong to swim/racket club that is part
of the Village foundation.

INCLUDES:

o CLUBHOUSE/REC. ROOM   3
o SWIMMING POOL (#5)
o TENNIS COURTS (#18)
o JACUZZI (#) ⎫
o SAUNA (#)   ⎬ + indoor pool Y.M.C.A. free
              ⎭   extra
o BIKEPATHS 12-13 miles
o FIELD GAMES
o OTHER Lake

MONTHLY ASSESSMENT: $175 Homes Corp.
                    parks
RECREATION FEE: $602 foundation
                swim/racket $ 86 volunteer
                           $235/yr. mand.

                           $321/yr. for swim/rack.

o MAINTENANCE OF EXTERIOR
● INSURANCE   (common space)
o WATER
● MAINT. COMMON SPACE
o OTHER: Lake main + street lights

BUYER PROFILE:

Average Age: 39 now 40-45
# of Children 2-3 (more than T.H.)
Average Income: $25,000 orig.
                    now $50,000

Prev. Residence: transfer from west
Both Spouses Work: no
Occupation Category: Prof. with
                    Blue Chip R&D Firms

FINANCING OFFERED:

o FHA   no
o VA   no

● CONVENTIONAL
o OTHER

SALES PROFILE AND HISTORY:
Date Opened: March, 1968
Weekly Sales Rate: 7-8 units week

Sold to Date: all
Total Unsold:

MATERIALS TO OBTAIN:

o Sales Brochure
o Price List
o Floor Plans
o Deed Restrictions
o Covenants

o Photographs
o Site Plan
o Approved Development Plan
o HOA Documents

INTERVIEWER: Jay Parker

Source: Bill Hurley

Development Concept
Planning Form

DEVELOPMENT: Four Seasons   DATE: 10/9/80
LOCATION: Ft. Collins, Colorado

     DATE OPENED: 2/80
DEVELOPER: Chism Homes, Inc.   DATE FINISHED:
           from Las Vegas

HOUSING CONCEPT: Zero lot line   ZONING: PUD
DENSITY: SETBACKS:
% OPEN SPACE: PROJECT SIZE:
ORGANIZATION OF OPEN SPACE: Greenbelts w/ trails   LOT SIZES: 58' wide x 110' deep

---

	(1)	(2)	(3)	(4)	(5)	(6)
PLAN #/NAME						
PRICE:	$74,500	$76,200	$69,900	$77,900	$78,100	$81,300
SQUARE FEET:		82,300	73,800			
# OF LEVELS	1 1/2	1	1	2	1 1/2	1 + loft
BEDROOMS	2	3	2	3 + den	2	3
BATHS	1 3/4	1 3/4	1 3/4	2	1 3/4	1 3/4
GARAGE	2-car	2-car	2-car	2-car	2-car	2-car

PLAN MIX

SOLD

PHYSICAL CHARACTER:

EXTERIOR:
   ROOF: Asphalt shingle
   SIDING: Frame, plywood and brick
   DRIVEWAY: 2 spaces in front of garage
   FENCING: Rear privacy
   LANDSCAPING: Front court
   SPRINKLERS:
   ARCH. TYPE: Traditional
   COLORS: orange

PLANNING FEATURES:
   PARKING: On street
   STREET LAYOUT: Cul de sac
   STREET WIDTHS:
   SPECIAL FEATURES:
   INNOVATIONS: 1st ZLL in Ft. Collins
   ENTRY:
   COMMON AREAS:
   IMAGE: Open fields surround, however
        is in rapidly growing sector
   BUILDING SEPARATIONS: of town
   ENERGY FEATURES:

Four Seasons

HOMEOWNERS ASSOCIATION: XXXXXXXXXX ASSESSMENT: $100/yr.
Fee the same for everyone in development   RECREATION FEE: (max. FHA allowed)
Zero Lot Line, conventional, etc.

INCLUDES:
   o CLUBHOUSE/REC. ROOM   o MAINTENANCE OF EXTERIOR
   o SWIMMING POOL (#)   o INSURANCE
   o TENNIS COURTS (#)   o WATER
   o JACUZZI (#)   o MAINT. COMMON SPACE
   o SAUNA (#)   o OTHER:
   o BIKEPATHS
   o FIELD GAMES
   ● OTHER   Greenbelt with pathways

BUYER PROFILE:
Average Age: 24-37 and 55-62
          Empty nesters   Prev. Residence: Local
# of Children   2 families out of 9 have young   Both Spouses Work: Yes
Average Income: children   Occupation Category: Professional
       $45,000-55,000 combined

FINANCING OFFERED:
   ● FHA   ● CONVENTIONAL
   ● VA   o OTHER

SALES PROFILE AND HISTORY:
Date Opened: 2/80   # Sold to Date: 17 under contract
Weekly Sales Rate: Total Unsold:

MATERIALS TO OBTAIN:
   ● Sales Brochure   ● Photographs
   ● Price List   ● Site Plan
   o Floor Plans   o Approved Development Plan
   o Deed Restrictions   o HOA Documents
   o Covenants

       INTERVIEWER: Gene Herbert

Development Concept
Planning Form

HOH Associates, Inc.

DEVELOPMENT: Country Walk
LOCATION: Dade County, Florida
DEVELOPER: Arvida Corp.

DATE: 8/80
DATE OPENED: 6/80
DATE FINISHED:

HOUSING CONCEPT: Zero Lot Line patio
DENSITY: 4.3
% OPEN SPACE: 40% min, required
ORGANIZATION OF OPEN SPACE:

ZONING: R4-1
SETBACKS: none required
PROJECT SIZE: 137 ac/596 d.u.
LOT SIZES: 55 x 80

PLAN #/NAME	(1) Ashville	(2) Glenville	(3) Oakville	(4) Woodville	(5)
PRICE:	$72,000	$77,000	$85,500	$93,500	$87,000
SQUARE FEET:	1,130	1,260	1,500	1,630	1,600
# OF LEVELS	1	1	1	2	1
BEDROOMS	2	3	3	3	3
BATHS	2	2	2	2	2
GARAGE	1-car	1-car	1-car	2-car	2-car
PLAN MIX	20%	23%	23%	23%	10%
# SOLD	47	62	49	29	10

PHYSICAL CHARACTER:

EXTERIOR:
  ROOF: asphalt shingles
  SIDING: masonite and weldwood
  DRIVEWAY: asphalt
  FENCING: horizontal shadowbox
  LANDSCAPING: yes - sod and 2-3 trees, 35± shrubs
  SPRINKLERS: yes
  ARCH. TYPE: New England Country
  COLORS: greys, blues, etc.

PLANNING FEATURES:
  PARKING: 3/du
  STREET LAYOUT: culs and loops
  STREET WIDTHS: 20' pavement
  SPECIAL FEATURES: reduced density, open space
  INNOVATIONS:
  ENTRY: Identification
  COMMON AREAS: Yes
  IMAGE: unique
  BUILDING SEPARATIONS:10' + 1-hr. wall
  ENERGY FEATURES:

Country Walk

HOMEOWNERS ASSOCIATION: Yes

MONTHLY ASSESSMENT: $27.50
RECREATION FEE: $25.00

INCLUDES:
 ● CLUBHOUSE/REC. ROOM (Cabana)
 ● SWIMMING POOL (#)
 ● TENNIS COURTS (#)
 ● JACUZZI (#)
 o SAUNA (#)
 ● BIKEPATHS
 ● FIELD GAMES minor areas
 ● OTHER amphitheater
          country store

 o MAINTENANCE OF EXTERIOR
 o INSURANCE
 o WATER
 ● MAINT. COMMON SPACE
 ● OTHER:
   24-hour patrol/covenants

BUYER PROFILE:
Average Age:
# of Children
Average Income:

Prev. Residence: Miami area
Both Spouses Work: 50% +
Occupation Category: Prof.

FINANCING OFFERED:
 o FHA
 o VA

 ● CONVENTIONAL
 o OTHER

SALES PROFILE AND HISTORY:
Date Opened: 6/7/80
Weekly Sales Rate: 39 +

Sold to Date: 596
Total Unsold: 375

MATERIALS TO OBTAIN:
 ● Sales Brochure
 ● Price List
 o Floor Plans
 o Deed Restrictions
 o Covenants

 ● Photographs
 o Site Plan
 ● Approved Development Plan
 o HOA Documents

INTERVIEWER: David R. Jensen

Development Concept
Planning Form

DEVELOPMENT: Cedarwood
LOCATION: Boca Raton, Florida

DEVELOPER: Coppolla Enterprises

DATE: 8/27/80

DATE OPENED: 4/77
DATE FINISHED: late 80

HOUSING CONCEPT: Zero Lot Line
DENSITY: 3.9 du/ac
% OPEN SPACE: none (it occurs in adj. areas)
ORGANIZATION OF OPEN SPACE:

ZONING: PUD
SETBACKS:15'F; 7½S; 10'Back
PROJECT SIZE: 9.3 ac/33 lots
LOT SIZES: 60 x 105

PLAN #/NAME	(1) Heron	(2) Sandpiper	(3) Seagull	(4) Pelican
PRICE:	$99,900	$106,400	$129,000	$123,600
SQUARE FEET:	1,830	2,015	2,500	2,300
# OF LEVELS	1	1	2	2
BEDROOMS	2	2+1	4+1	3
BATHS	2	2	2½	2½
GARAGE	2-car	2-car	2-car	2-car
PLAN MIX # SOLD	2	18	12	1

PHYSICAL CHARACTER:

EXTERIOR:
  ROOF: cedar shake
  SIDING: cedar plywood
  DRIVEWAY: exp. aggregate
  FENCING: cedar (open, 1 x 3 on edge)
  LANDSCAPING: $4,300 allocation/unit
  SPRINKLERS: yes
  ARCH. TYPE: mixed
  COLORS: gray stain with earth trim

PLANNING FEATURES:
  PARKING: 2 garage/2 drive
  STREET LAYOUT: cul de sacs
  STREET WIDTHS: 42 ROW/20pave.
  SPECIAL FEATURES: Landscape Islands
  INNOVATIONS:
  ENTRY: Village Identification
  COMMON AREAS: lake edge landscaping
  IMAGE:
  BUILDING SEPARATIONS:
  ENERGY FEATURES:

Cedarwood
HOMEOWNERS ASSOCIATION: Master Assoc.

MONTHLY ASSESSMENT: $75.00
RECREATION FEE:

INCLUDES:
  o CLUBHOUSE/REC. ROOM   Separate
  o SWIMMING POOL (#)   Club
  o TENNIS COURTS (#)   Membership
  o JACUZZI (#)
  o SAUNA (#)
  o BIKEPATHS
  o FIELD GAMES
  o OTHER

  ● MAINTENANCE OF EXTERIOR
  ● INSURANCE
  ● WATER
  ● MAINT. COMMON SPACE
  ● OTHER: Landscape maintenance

BUYER PROFILE:
Average Age: 55
# of Children 2½
Average Income: $100,000 +

Prev. Residence: out of state
Both Spouses Work: no
Occupation Category: Executive and
                          Entrepreneurs

FINANCING OFFERED:
  o FHA
  o VA

  ● CONVENTIONAL
  ● OTHER

SALES PROFILE AND HISTORY:
Date Opened: 4/77
Weekly Sales Rate:

Sold to Date: 36
Total Unsold: None

MATERIALS TO OBTAIN:
  ● Sales Brochure
  ● Price List
  ● Floor Plans
  o Deed Restrictions
  o Covenants

  o Photographs
  o Site Plan
  o Approved Development Plan
  o HOA Documents

INTERVIEWER: David R. Jensen

List of Figures

Bibliography

Engstrom, Robert and Putman, Marc. *Planning and Design of Townhouses and Condominiums.* Washington, D.C.: Urban Land Institute; 1979.

Kelly, George. *Rocky Mountain Horticulture.* Boulder, Colorado: Pruett Press, 1967.

Munzer, Martha E. *Planning Our Town.* New York: Alfred A. Knopf, 1964.

The Pros and Cons of Cluster Housing. Washington, D.C.: Urban Land Institute, 1968.

Residential Development Handbook. Washington, D.C.: Urban Land Institute, 1978.

Robinette, Gary O. *Handbook of Landscape Architectural Construction: Pavement in the Landscape.* McLean, Virginia: The Landscape Architectural Foundation, Inc., 1976.

Schoenaur, Norbert and Seaman, Stanley. *The Court-Garden House.* Montreal: McGill University Press, 1962.

Shomon, Joseph James. *Open Land for Urban America.* Baltimore: The Johns Hopkins Press, 1971.

White, William H. *Cluster Development.* New York: Woodhaven Press Associates Corporation, 1967.

Wittausch, William K. *The Patio House.* Washington, D.C.: Urban Land Institute, 1963.